Not Forgotten

NOT FORGOTTEN

The Story of an Extraordinary Woman

Angela Byrne

NEW ISLAND

NOT FORGOTTEN
First published 2011
by New Island
2 Brookside
Dundrum Road
Dublin 14
www.newisland.ie

ISBN 978-1-8484-0128-0

British Library Cataloguing Data. A CIP catalogue record for this book is available from the British Library

Printed by Tìšín Printing House

New Island received financial assistance from
The Arts Council (An Comhairle Ealaíon), Dublin, Ireland

10 9 8 7 6 5 4 3 2 1

Dedicated to Kitty's memories

For my husband, John, and our children:
Lisa, John-James, Noel and Declan.

Thank you to my sister
Maura for her contributions and research.

Contents

Preface

Years ago a young mother sat with her dying aunt who begged her to fetch a notebook and pen so that she could write down the details of her family history. The old woman insisted that she should know the full story because she was sure that one day her niece would want to write a book about it. To humour her aunt, the young woman did as she was asked.

I was that young woman and my aunt's words resonated through the years after her death until I finally came to realise that my family's story was indeed extraordinary. However it is also, sadly, a typical tale of the Irish diaspora: of fortunes sought, quiet lives torn by separation, loves lost and heart-rending reunions. The story haunted me until finally, one day, I was driven to my computer to record the history of my grandfather Oliver's betrayal of my grandmother, Nora, and the impact that this betrayal had on the life of his daughter, my most unusual Aunt Kitty.

*

When I was a little girl I found Aunt Kitty difficult and even bad-tempered sometimes. My first memory of her is from when I was very small and she came to take care of me and my siblings when my mother, Betty, was ill. I missed my mother desperately and could not accept the stern Aunt Kitty. But when I grew up and became more patient and thoughtful, I became fascinated with the stories that Kitty had to tell, with her powers of recall and insight into her own life and the society that she grew up in. I have preserved her stories as much as possible in the pages that follow, adding information gleaned from old family letters and records and the memories of our mutual relatives, as well as official sources such as libraries and archives, many of which are now available online. However, most of what you are about to read is Kitty's own testimony, taken both from my memories of conversations with her over the years and those notes that she requested I make in the leather-bound notebook. I have changed all of the names in the text to protect the privacy of our surviving relatives.

This is the story of events that took place from the 1920s onwards in a small, quite ordinary, Irish town – events that have reverberated down through the generations of our family. But it is more particularly the story of one young Irish girl, Kitty, and how she grew up and reached womanhood under the most challenging and difficult of circumstances. It describes how she confronted the many obstacles in her path with all the resources available to her at a time when money was scarce, girls were expected to do what they were told, and opportunity was only there for the fearless. It is about how Kitty lived her life to the full and how, when the right moment came, she looked straight into the eyes of the person who had hurt her the most and confronted her own deepest fears, sorrows and anguish.

To a lesser extent, this book is also about us, the younger generations of her family, for whom Kitty has been an inspiration and a source of knowledge and insight not just about our own background, but also about an Ireland that has vanished and will never be seen again. We feel no nostalgia for this long-gone Ireland since, imperfect as things are today for most people and certainly for this family, they are still immeasurably better than they were then.

Angela Byrne
Kilkenny, October 2011

Kitty with her dog Brandy, Templemore Co. Tipperary

Prologue

Picture the Manchester Palais dance hall on Valentine's Day 1919 – the first Valentine's Day after the end of the Great War. Four young girls from Tipperary notice a rather dashing stranger walking towards them and their hearts begin to pound as they look at each other and wonder which girl is about to get lucky. Oliver McManus is by far the finest man in the room that night and in just a few moments it will be Nora Langley's life that he turns upside down forever.

'Will you dance?' he asks, holding out his hand in the expectation that she will accept his invitation because Oliver has never been turned down by a girl before.

Hesitating for just a fraction of a moment, she smiles a breathless 'yes', puts her smaller hand into his and follows him onto the floor where scores of couples are already swaying to the latest dance tunes. 'It' has happened – and the electricity between the two is palpable. Nora melts into Oliver's arms and they dance all night: slow dances, the foxtrot, quicksteps, the waltz and a few Irish dances for good measure. They seem bewitched by each other. Mary, Alice and Margaret, Nora's friends, are intrigued too. Although they are all asked up onto the floor themselves, they cannot help sneaking glances in the direction of their rapt friend and her handsome partner. Who *is* this stranger that seems to have swept her off her feet? Where has he come from, and what are his intentions?

After the dance Oliver walks Nora and her friends home. When they reach the girls' boarding house he is quite forward, asking if he can come in for a cup of tea and a cigarette so as to enjoy their company for a little longer. Nora agrees, of course. How can she resist? After all, she has her friends as chaperones and she can hardly bear to say goodbye to this captivating young gentleman.

The five young people sit up all night talking and smoking and drinking cups of tea. Oliver is full of stories about his time in France during the war, life in the trenches, and his heroic ability to get both himself and his friends out of life-threatening situations. He is, he assures them, a brilliant marksman, and it is because of this that he has survived and made it through against all the odds. What the girls do not know is that his ability to spin a tale has always made him popular company amongst his peers and enthralling young women is his favourite pastime. He has these four pretty friends eating from the palm of his hand tonight, captivated with his tales of derring-do and begging him for more until the room brightens to a grey, cold dawn.

Later that morning, with the dew still shining on the black railings outside the house, Oliver bids Nora farewell at the bottom of the stairs to the building. 'Will you come to the pictures with me tomorrow night?' he asks. 'It would make me very happy indeed if you would say "yes"'.

'I will,' Nora says, with a blush. 'You can meet me here after seven, when I'm home from work.'

Inside the house her friends are breathlessly waiting for a report on those vital last words – and more than a little envious when they hear that there is a satisfying outcome. They chatter excitedly for a while like four sparrows and eventually go to bed to sleep for an hour or two.

'What a night this has been,' Nora thinks, staring from her bedroom window at the rustling, bare branches of the February trees shaking off the darkness in preparation for a chilly spring day. 'Who would have imagined that I might meet the love of my life on an ordinary night out with the girls?' She cannot believe her luck and is already quite sure that Oliver will prove to be a very important person to her indeed. She has no inkling of his infamy back home in Tipperary, or any idea of the devastating effect that his easy socialising and winning way with the ladies will have on her future.

1

A long way from there to here

In those wild years after the war Manchester thronged with young Irish looking for a brighter future and they naturally gravitated to socialising with each other, feeling a strong sense of camaraderie as the Irish always do when they travel abroad to live and work. Travel was expensive and time-consuming and homesickness common, so it was comforting to spend time talking about what was going on back home and read letters aloud so that all the news could be shared. Being part of this small community gave them a real sense that they had arrived in a 'home from home' and that there was continuity between their old lives in Ireland and Manchester's grimy streets.

When Oliver McManus chose to return to civilian life in Manchester after the horror of the French trenches, his natural charm made him exceptionally popular in the Irish community and so his whirlwind romance with Nora Langley rapidly became the latest 'hot news'. Their friends all thought them the perfect match: they were both in their early twenties, exceptionally attractive, from the same part of Ireland, and with steady incomes that gave them a means to express their *joie de vivre* and to kick up their heels a little.

*

Since Oliver was the eldest son of a successful tradesman in the small market town of Templemore in County Tipperary, his prospects were better than those of many thousands of his peers and in 1912 there had been no pressing need for him to leave home and enlist in the British army. His parents had married in 1893 and Oliver had been born a year later on 28 November 1894. Another four boys and four girls followed over a twenty-four-year period (Victor, Kate, Maggie, Richard, Noreen, Peter, Kevin and Connie) until his mother's swansong, the sixth and youngest boy, Jack. There may have been ten children but there was always plenty to eat and drink and their home, although modest enough, was still a warm and comfortable place.

As a child Oliver was a model son, bright, obedient and clever. He attended the local Christian Brothers' school where he did quite well and he served as an altar boy at Mass seven days a week. Weddings and funerals were his favourites because the altar boys were always slipped a little money along with the priests and the sacristan. He was a picture in his robes – but there was a mischievous glint in his eye as he walked up the aisle, hinting that he was not always the saintly child that he appeared.

When he left school at fourteen he went straight into the cobbler's workshop to assist his father. In those days few girls or boys persisted in school beyond that age because they were needed to contribute to the income of the household, further education being a luxury that only the very wealthy could afford. Oliver was quick to pick up the art of shoemaking and was as efficient as many adults while still only a teenager. His parents considered him a paragon, but the glint in the altar boy's eye was merely the tip of the iceberg. He had a talent for mischief and a quick way with words that made him instantly popular with other children. In 1908, at the age of fourteen, he was caught and fined by the British authorities for playing handball in the street (the sport was banned by the British government of the time for its nationalist associations).

This event was duly reported in the local newspaper. It was neither the first, nor would it be the last, time that a McManus made local headlines, no doubt to the private delight and entertainment of their neighbours. Well-respected locally they may have been, but there was a wild streak running through the clan that got them into a lot of trouble. In 1903, Martin McManus, Oliver's father, had assaulted a farm labourer. The newspaper reported that the attack had happened after the labourer insulted one of McManus' friends. Martin McManus was known (or least liked to be known) as the tough man who was fierce and would back down from nothing. He believed in friendship and commanded respect, but beneath this outer show he was violent by nature and had a tendency to land himself in situations such as this when rushing to the defence of his friends.

At the time the family must have been better off than most of its neighbours and Martin certainly considered himself to be an honourable man. However, he seems to have been struggling to make ends meet because he began stealing and became increasingly involved in fights. Or perhaps the ten mouths at home had little to do with it, and the reality was that the adventure and challenge of going out to steal for them actually gave him a thrill.

Whatever the truth, he began to teach his sons do the same. Unfortunately none of them were very good at it and had a nasty habit of being caught in the act. In 1906 Oliver's brother Victor was accused of stealing turkeys from a local woman – he would have been less than twelve years old at the time. Victor was arrested, sent to court and fined. In 1908, around the same time as the handball fine, Martin brought Oliver with him to steal timber from the local landlord's property. They were caught by the rich man's gamekeeper and a tussle ensued.

In 1916, four years after Oliver himself had enlisted, the *Nenagh Guardian* reported that Oliver's younger sister Kate (just fifteen at the time) had been involved in a fracas with other women on the street and was required to give testimony before a local magistrate. Leaving aside Oliver's mother, Mary, the McManus women were as 'lively' a bunch as the males of the family and were often to be seen in court for fighting and causing trouble. There was not much to do in Templemore and Kate and her friends liked to hang out on the main street, drinking and looking for anything to pass the time, including the odd argument or fight for entertainment's sake. They were girls who owned virtually nothing but liked to fight over what little they did have. Moreover they enjoyed watching their friends fight and would provoke each other with bitchy remarks and rumours.

In spite of all of this, loving and caring as she was, Mary McManus continued to back her children up, sort out their problems and believe they could do no wrong. Between their father encouraging them to steal and their mother turning a blind eye, the wilful McManus children must have thought they could get away with murder. But if the children took advantage of Mary's gentle disposition and fierce loyalty, Martin was even worse. It seems that he was prone to taking out his frustrations on his wife and, in the same year as Kate appeared in court, there came an attack that went one step too far for Mary. She determined to stop the beatings. The local newspaper stated that Mary McManus had gone to the guards to report that her husband had assaulted her, but had then changed her mind when the case came to court, testifying that he had been in the throes of an epileptic fit and not in full knowledge of what he was doing. Perhaps she was worried that Martin would be brought to jail and she left with all the mouths to feed, so she made up a little story that would keep him out of prison.

Although the children grew up in a violent home they stuck by each other. Mary had reported her husband to the guards, but the couple still stayed together. Whenever Martin or any of the McManuses appeared in court all his friends would go to support him, cheering and roaring and clapping him on the back if he got off. Martin had loyal friends and a close-knit family – and he knew it.

*

When he joined the army on 3 December 1912, Oliver was just eighteen years old and a citizen of a country that was still part of the United Kingdom. He imagined that he had bought himself a front-row ticket to all the drama and glamour that was rightfully his – a life far away from the small-town claustrophobia of Templemore. When Britain entered World War One on 4 August 1914, hundreds more young Irishmen enlisted but it was rarely nationalism that drove them. Many were simply in search of the decent income they could not find in their home towns or were, like Oliver, chasing youth's dream to leave home and see a bit of the world. Some of his compatriots were as young as fifteen when they reached the killing fields of Europe, having lied on their enlistment papers. Whatever their age, the catch phrase on everyone's lips was 'home by Christmas' and the expectation was that mortality rates would be low. No one had bargained on the trauma of the conflict that was to follow.

Once in France's muddy, rat-infested trenches it became clear that the war was emphatically *not* going to be over by Christmas; it would not be over for several Christmases to come and millions of young men, many not yet out of their teens, would shed their blood before the end came. A huge proportion of the Irish boys who had joined the British army, so full of expectations for a bright future, never went home at all or went back to wives and families who could barely recognise them – with missing limbs, faces burned beyond recognition and emotional scars that, although invisible, would never heal.

For those left alive in the trenches it also rapidly became clear that leaving the army was going to be infinitely more difficult than joining it. The penalty for desertion or for refusing to fight, which was seen as cowardice, was summary execution. Many of the young men who were executed by the British army for desertion were suffering from what was then known as 'shell shock', today referred to as 'post-traumatic stress syndrome'.

Oliver had quite a successful military career. By the end of the war he was twenty-four but he had already attained the rank of sergeant by the time he was nineteen, a considerable achievement at that age. He brought two medals for bravery back from the front with him, the first of these awarded for pulling two young, seriously wounded men from the trenches and dragging them to safety. One of the two was in danger of bleeding to death and Oliver had saved his life by cutting up his own uniform to tie around his friend's leg and staunch the flow. Having saved the one, he immediately turned to the other and administered 'the kiss of life', bringing him back to consciousness. Oliver went on to risk his own life on many occasions with no apparent fear or concern for his own well-being. Comradeship within one's regiment was particularly important for the Irish recruits; they were so frequently seen as mere cannon fodder that the bond between fellow soldiers was often all that stood between a man and death. Whatever shortcomings he may have demonstrated in later life, you could not fault Oliver as a soldier.

*

The Irish war casualties were quickly forgotten by the free Irish State that emerged in the post-war years. It considered them traitors and refused to acknowledge their great sacrifice – a sacrifice often made in the belief that their efforts would help to remove their families from the poverty that was so widespread in Ireland. But many of the so-called survivors were also casualties. These men were maimed on the front and received long-term treatment in English hospitals; often they remained in England for the rest of their lives knowing that they were no longer welcome at home.

The rest were flung back into ordinary life without any recognition of the challenges that they had faced on the battlefield and the trauma they had endured. They were men grown unaccustomed to the daily stresses of life. For years their commanding officer had taken decisions on their behalf and all that had been asked of them was that they rose, ate and slept at preordained times and did exactly as they were told. Many of these survivors,

Oliver among them, may not have lost their lives or limbs, but they surely must have lost a piece of their souls. To his friends he seemed unscarred by his experiences, almost like a man who had just been on holiday, but it is possible that Oliver's casual air was his way of covering up his reaction to the terror and torment of those dreadful years. Or perhaps the horror simply spurred him on, like so many others in the post-war years, to live life to the full after witnessing so much death.

Whatever he felt inside, at the close of the war Oliver, like his peers, had to decide where and how he would pick up the tattered shreds of his previous life. Having seen something of the world now, he certainly did not feel very inclined to return to Templemore. It was a beautiful small town and there were times when he missed it and longed to be with his family or coursing dogs with his friends, but he also wanted to live the high life and sample the pubs and dance halls in Manchester for a while before returning to his homeland.

Soon Oliver knew the streets of Manchester and every pub and dance hall frequented by the Irish like the back of his hand. He liked to have a good time and he knew how to go about finding one. Working hours were long and men and women alike were expected to work very hard in return for modest salaries in those years, so the young people longed for the weekends when a little fun and laughter in the dance halls gave them the opportunity to wind down. Drinking played a big role in the social life of the city just as it had in Ireland, but because alcoholic drinks were not allowed into the halls, the men were in the habit of taking several pints beforehand. Arriving slightly drunk had the added advantage of giving them the courage they needed to ask the girls to dance. Finally they were living the dream that had kept them going through those dark months in the trenches and they intended to make the most of it.

Many of these nervous ex-soldiers back in Manchester's dance halls were a little shy around girls. Not so Oliver, whose good looks even as a small child had left him with plenty of confidence. From the age of twelve or so he had grown accustomed to the giggling attention of girls and accepted it as his due. As vain as he was handsome, he spent whatever spare money he had on buying the latest suits and ties, since clothing was his biggest passion in life after girls. And his efforts paid off: Oliver always had more girlfriends than he knew what to do with. Rumour has it that even in France he had run true to character and had fathered children, although nobody knows how many or with whom. One of the main attractions of a big city like Manchester, as he saw it, was that it was easier to persuade girls to come to bed with him for a night of fun without any consequences than it would be in a small town like Templemore. Women – married or single – were his weakness and he never tried to resist the charms of a pretty face.

*

Going out in the big city of Manchester was very exciting for twenty-one-year-old Nora and she was just beginning to savour her freedom when she chanced to meet Oliver. Her background in a quiet rural community of Tipperary was quite different from his. She had been raised in Ballycurran, in a house nestled alongside the country road that led from Thurles to Holy Cross. Her father, Tom Langley, was a village schoolmaster at the Ballinakill National School. He was a tough father but his family had benefited from the decent wage that he brought home every week and from his insistence that all eight of his children – Jack, Thomas, Nora, Josie, Mairead, Maggie, Alice and Cathy – acquire a good standard of learning, so that they knew enough about the world and their place in it to sally forth with confidence. Tom's wife, Ellen, supported his views. She was very ambitious for her children and anxious that the girls, in particular, should grow up to make good matches with respectable men from the area. Consequently, they never lacked for anything as children and there was even money enough to send the girls for singing and piano lessons.

Throughout childhood Nora rewarded her father's insistence by being quiet, diligent, studious and obedient. She was determined that she would build a comfortable and prosperous life for herself by her own efforts. At the time she left school there was little work available locally and she went to a wealthy farmer as housekeeper, cooking and cleaning for the family and their two farm labourers, as well as sometimes minding the farmer's five children. Although she was only eighteen she had already begun to feel tired and trapped by her long hours and never-ending workload. Since she rarely even had time to snatch a bite to eat, she also began to lose weight. Looking on, her parents were increasingly concerned and disappointed that their clever daughter was working as a glorified servant for very little money, especially given their aspirations for their children. They urged Nora to find another job but it was clear to her that she would have to leave Ireland. Three of her close friends (Mary, Alice and Margaret) had already gone to England and Nora's plan was to save enough money to join them, although on her impossibly low wages it looked as if this might take a lifetime.

Finally, she asked her parents for her fare to England, which resulted in an almighty row. They most certainly did not want her to go, particularly her father who expected that all his children would stay in Tipperary, even though emigration seemed to be the only way forward for an ambitious young Irish person at that time. But after a week or so her mother approached her and said confidentially, 'Go, Nora, and make a life for yourself. Don't tell your father about this, he doesn't know I have a little put away for the rainy day. You know how he would be, he would want it to get more drink and then be just awful to us all.' With that she offered her daughter enough money for Nora's fare and for accommodation when she arrived.

Grateful and amazed that her mother should have managed to hide money away from her father, Nora immediately contacted her friends in England and made arrangements to leave Ballycurran. The day she left home was mixed with delight and sadness. As she kissed her brothers, sisters and parents goodbye, she comforted everyone by telling them she would write as soon as she landed in England and would soon save enough money to sail back and take them all shopping for new clothes.

It all happened just as she had hoped. A new, promising job in a bank opened up for her as soon as she arrived in Manchester and she began to savour life away from her own small town. And then she met Oliver. How different things might have been if she and her friends had chosen a different dance hall that Valentine's night.

2

The course of true love

Nora and Oliver's romance blossomed on the dance floor. Dance halls were a favourite venue for the couples of the time, since the act of dancing brought the opportunity for an intimacy that many were unlikely to experience in an age when 'courting' couples were usually still chaperoned. The Palais remained their favourite dance hall, as it was with all the young Irish, but because it was rather expensive it was saved for special occasions, such as when an Irish céilí band was visiting. Ballroom music impresario Victor Silvester was often to be heard there, too, and it was seen as a slightly exclusive venue, not just because of the price but also because a suit and tie rule was enforced on the door. Many a young Irishman was turned away with a 'Sorry sir, not tonight. Suit and tie only.'

After they met, Nora and Oliver often contented themselves with going to the local dance hall instead of the costly Palais. Although no alcohol was available at any of the halls, refreshments were served in the form of tea or orange squash and perhaps some sandwiches or biscuits. Most had balconies where these refreshments could be enjoyed while watching the dancers on the floor below and catching up on all the latest gossip.

But it hardly seemed to matter where they went. Night after night that spring Oliver called for Nora and sometimes they simply walked through the streets of Manchester or out along the river. Nora was happier than she had ever been in her life. She relished being on the arm of a handsome young suitor who seemed to want nothing more than to make her happy and she could not help but appreciate the envious glances that she attracted. Despite the griminess of Manchester's streets, the daffodils were in bloom, birds were busy chattering and nest-building overhead, and the evening air was cool and fresh. When the young couple grew tired, they sat on one of the park benches to rest for a moment or two before moving on again.

Manchester's parks were splendid but Oliver assured Nora that they were nothing to compare with the beautiful park that ran through his home town, Templemore, past the quaint houses and along the lakeside where local men fished for trout and perch in the evenings. Nora had been in Templemore before, but Oliver made her feel as though she knew it like the back of her hand, just as he did. He painted a picture of the elegant church with its grounds, the busy main street and the striking town hall and told her of woods, rivers and castles nearby – she thought it sounded like the most wonderful place on earth.

Walking with Nora on his arm Oliver convinced himself that she was the love of his life and that they could be happy together forever. He thought he might be able to set aside his philandering ways and be faithful to this beautiful woman who was clearly very much in love with him. After all, he had managed to survive the war, could giving up his womanising really be more difficult?

It was not just the spell of Nora's graceful neck, long-lashed eyes and lily-white complexion that increasingly bound Oliver – she had other virtues to draw him in. Thanks to a combination of natural talent and her years of music studies, she had a fine, haunting voice that she was not afraid to use publicly. Whenever she performed she captivated her audience and a pin could have been heard to drop. 'You sing just like an angel,' she was often told, and she was frequently assured in the next breath that if she had chosen to pursue a career in music she could have been famous. But she had no interest in anything other than using her voice for the pleasure of her friends and family. Oliver was falling for the voice as much as the face and, as their relationship developed, he often asked her to sing for him or for a small group of their friends. She usually obliged, fully conscious that she was wooing her man. Mesmerised, he listened and watched until he was sure he was ready to commit body and soul to this one woman.

*

One night in late March Oliver turned up out of the blue, dressed to impress in a new suit, shirt and tie. His hair was cut and groomed to perfection and his moustache had been neatly trimmed. Nora answered the knock on the door full of excitement at meeting her lover, her man – and immediately she saw him she realised this was to be no ordinary night. She gazed shyly straight into his eyes, then took his arm and, humming a happy little tune of nervousness and anticipation, walked out with Oliver to meet their friends.

Despite his eagerness Oliver held back for just the right moment to say his piece. When the music stopped so that the band could take a break, he seized his opportunity and, in front of all their friends, he went down on one knee before her.

'Nora,' he said in a husky voice as he reached out for her hand. 'Will you do me the great honour of agreeing to become my wife?'

Oliver waited for Nora to assent. It had never occurred to him that she might not; no woman had ever said 'no' to him.

Nora had imagined Oliver saying these words since the night they had met. In quiet moments she had found herself writing 'Mrs Nora McManus' over and over again and then, half-embarrassed, had torn the paper up and thrown it in the fire. She had not even confided these slightly embarrassing fantasies to her friends. Now her heart raced. The precious time was here and she felt a little tear of joy roll down her face. But no words came out, in spite of the way that she had rehearsed this scene endlessly in her mind's eye. She opened her mouth and out came only a small squeak of a 'yes'. Oliver leapt to his feet and threw his arms around her to seal their agreement with a kiss that lasted just a little too long for propriety and ended when their friends started cat-calling and laughing, 'You're not married yet, you know!'

When they turned to face their companions it seemed that half of Irish Manchester was there to cheer the popular couple, so terrific was the noise of the stamping and tumultuous the flinging of caps in the air. Everyone bought rounds of drinks and toasted the couple with 'Long life, happiness and many children!' All night long Nora and Oliver danced, sang and dreamed of the future. Later Nora blushed when Oliver whispered in her ear of the large family that their friends had wished them. They would be happy forever; they were both sure of it.

Nora and Oliver might now be engaged but there was still no question of their ever being alone together, although he often spent almost the whole night in her boarding house entertaining all four girls, just as he had on the first night, with his yarns of France and Ireland. Nora was fiercely proud of her reputation. In those days a girl's reputation could be damaged after just a few hours alone in a young man's company and she knew that she was lucky to have Mary, Alice and Margaret to chaperone them. The other girls saw the young couple kiss and touch each other affectionately, but nothing more. The happiness that seemed to radiate from the pair made each one long to find a man who would make her feel that she was the only woman in the world.

*

Carried away by all the excitement, Nora started making wedding plans immediately. Her friends and housemates had watched every glorious moment of her romance since the first night and now the four girls spent their evenings poring over dress patterns and swatches of fabric. Although Nora knew that she would have very little money to spend on her wedding outfit, she was determined to be as stylish as possible because the man she was going to marry deserved to have a wife who was truly beautiful. She also wrote immediately to her parents to tell them the wonderful news that their daughter was to be married to a Tipperary man.

She had been quite convinced that they would be delighted to hear about this handsome Irishman from their own area who had swept her off her feet and that her family would welcome him with open arms when she finally brought him back to Thurles. Especially as she had been warned, quite sternly, that it was out of the question for her to bring an Englishman home and that, when it came to choosing a husband, it was particularly important that he be a good Catholic and preferably an Irish one. Marrying outside one's culture and faith was very much frowned upon. Such marriages were referred to as 'mixed' and the young couple was often disowned by both sides of the family.

However, instead of the excited letter of congratulations that Nora expected, back came word that her parents wanted her to return to Ireland straight away and that she should not make any wedding plans as her father had an altogether different arrangement in mind for her.

'Cut off your relationship with this man,' Nora, was instructed, 'because he's no good for you. We have something else in mind, so be a good girl and mind your parents.'

Unbeknownst to Nora, Tom had long planned for her to wed a well-to-do, well-educated local farmer. Although considerably older, this man was (Tom judged) an excellent catch for his pretty, refined young daughter. He had let her go to Manchester to work so that she could experience a year or two of freedom before settling down with this stable husband who would, he felt, give her the safe home that Tom believed she needed. Not to mention help out with dowries for the rest of the Langley daughters. Love or attraction did not come into it: as far as Tom was concerned land and money provided a better basis for a good relationship than simple emotions. Tom could see nothing wrong with this plan and felt that he had been an excellent father in landing such a good catch for his daughter. He also appeared quite confident that Nora would do as she was told: 'We are expecting you on the next boat over,' his letter read. 'Come home as soon as possible and we will speak no more of this foolishness of yours.'

Nora wept bitter tears to read her father's words. She loved her parents and she had never expected them to have any opposition to her engagement. Instead she had imagined them rejoicing at her good fortune and sharing the great news with the rest of the family. In her mind's eye she had seen her sisters' excitement, the fights over who would be bridesmaid and herself walking up the aisle on her father's arm, turning to kiss him fondly on the cheek before he gave her away.

There was another reason for this arranged marriage, a reason that her parents never explained to Nora. Two of Nora's sisters, Cathy and Maggie, had moved to Dublin to find work after Nora had set off for Manchester. This set alarm bells ringing with the Langleys who realised it was more than likely that the remaining siblings would also be forced away from home in search of work. Tom was not a particularly healthy man and, although he was not yet old, he could sense his energies waning and felt that he might need a lot of care in his later years. Nora had always been a kind and gentle girl and she seemed the most appropriate choice as caregiver. What was more, Tom reasoned that if she was married to a much older man she would not be likely to have a large family and would have more time to spend worrying about the needs of her parents. In securing marriage to an older local farmer for Nora, Tom Langley had also hoped to ensure that he and his wife would be well taken care of in old age.

But he had seriously underestimated their daughter's determination. Nora tore the letter up and ignored her parents' orders. She had no intention of giving up her man for another whom she neither knew nor wished to know. She hated the thought of her father selling her hand in marriage to the highest bidder and was disgusted by the notion that he might be after her prospective husband's money. Instead she speeded up preparations for the wedding, since she was now determined to marry Oliver as quickly as possible, sure that she would never regret taking the decision to become his wife. Nora reasoned also that if she were to become pregnant as soon as she was wed she could present her parents with a fait accompli and they would have no choice but to accept her wonderful husband. Eventually, she was sure, they would come to love and appreciate him too. Oliver was charming, entertaining and ebullient. Nora felt that if her parents spent any time with him they would enjoy his stories about the war and notice his positive attributes. She also believed that her parents would be impressed that he had an established trade as a shoemaker, one that he was good at and at which his family had made a successful living.

The idea of a quick, quiet wedding suited Oliver too. They could not afford a big affair and he was an impatient man, eager to get his pretty bride into bed. Never before had he waited this long before a conquest and he was not adapting well to the waiting game.

*

On 20 April 1919 Nora and Oliver were married at eight in the morning in their local church in Manchester. It was a fresh day, but the sun was just creeping through the clouds as the groom made his way into the church past grassy banks sprinkled with the yellow flowers of spring. Inside, a small wedding party of the couple's friends waited for the beautiful bride to enter. Nora was ten minutes late. The priest was becoming uneasy and so was Oliver. Morning Mass could not be delayed and there were already local parishioners in the church, there for daily worship.

The bride finally arrived with Alice and Margaret, her two bridesmaids. The two friends wore light pink coat dresses, with pretty headdresses and shoes to match, and carried bouquets of pink and white roses. In lieu of her father, who was still furious with her and had refused to attend in the hope that she would change her mind, Oliver's best friend, Martin, was there to give Nora away.

The groom was kneeling at the front of the nave when Nora entered. He turned to see his bride at the same moment as the wedding party stood to watch her walk slowly and carefully up the aisle. Nora had dreamed of making the most of her limited budget and she had unquestionably succeeded. She wore a magnificent coat of the most delicate lavender colour, a dress to match, and a box hat of the same material with a little mesh veil that covered her eyes. She had chosen the ensemble with the help of her friends, buying the coat and hat, but sewing the dress herself, each tiny stitch in the fine fabric made painstakingly with love and anticipation of her new life. Her shoes and bag were of shiny black patent, and her gloves of fine black leather fitted like a second skin, making her tiny hands appear even more slender and delicate. She held a small, simple bouquet of six white roses with some maidenhair fern trailing down in the middle. Her dark brown hair was done in the latest style – shoulder length, with a slight curl at the ends – and it framed her face perfectly, making her look almost absurdly young for a bride. She wore just a dusting of powder, a bit of rouge on her cheeks and the faintest colouring of red on her lips. Assessing herself in the mirror earlier that morning before leaving the flat, she had thought, 'Yes, Oliver will like me like this.' Already she had understood how important it was to Oliver that she should always look her best and her unspoken wedding vow was that, even in pregnancy, she would always look attractive for her new husband.

And, indeed, Oliver did like what he saw. Her natural good taste ensured that she was as pretty as a picture when she came up the aisle towards him. The wedding Mass was brief and within half an hour Oliver and Nora had been made man and wife, bound to each other for the rest of their natural days. The priest's homily advised the couple to take seriously God's wish for them, which he described as acceptance of whatever children the Creator saw fit to send and the raising of these children within the Catholic faith. Nora and Oliver solemnly promised to be good parents and to raise their offspring within the church and with all due regard for the importance of Catholic teachings.

Outside the church the day was beginning to warm up and the wedding guests relaxed in the sun, exchanging admiring comments about the young couple. Some photographs were taken quickly – just one or two, as photographs were very expensive – and then their friends threw confetti over the newly-weds. For a few brief moments doubt scurried across Nora's mind. 'What about my parents back in Thurles? I told them that I was getting married today. Are they thinking about me?' She looked at the brightly coloured wedding confetti on the dark ground. 'Will we still be happy when the colour has faded from the confetti? Will my parents accept us? Surely they will. Probably they have already sent us a telegram with good wishes for lifelong happiness and prosperity. And, if not, no doubt the best man will read a card from them at the wedding breakfast.'

Her thoughts also flew to her brothers and sisters. None of them had written. Was she in their thoughts? She would have dearly loved her sisters with her as bridesmaids and she knew that they would have adored choosing and wearing the pretty dresses and creating fancy hairdos. Nora shook her head. Where were these negative thoughts coming from? Then the happy cries and cheers of her friends called her back to the present.

The reception was held in a local hotel where a friend of Oliver's had thrown his own wedding reception a few months earlier. That couple, too, had had a small, quick wedding – and directly after the reception they had returned to the groom's home town in Ireland to settle into married life. Impressed by what the hotel had to offer and even more taken by the fact that it was inexpensive, Oliver had quickly made all the arrangements to celebrate their own wedding there. Just like their friends before them, Nora and Oliver were showered with gifts. However, at this point it became clear that Oliver did not want the similarity to his friends' marriage ending there. To Nora's shock he presented her with two boat tickets back to Ireland. He had harboured a dream, it seemed, that both would return to Templemore after the wedding and that he would go back into the family business. He believed their move home would be another adventure and that they would return as the successful young couple, admired by family and friends. They would be returning on a high.

To say that Nora was not impressed would be an understatement. But she was particularly horrified by the idea that Oliver clearly considered this to be his wedding present to her. Never before had he discussed the possibility that they might go back to Ireland. While she loved her homeland and had often missed her friends and family, she adored the freedom that her new life in Manchester offered, as well as the good salary she earned at the bank. She had grown very independent and used to making her own decisions. What would it be like, having to depend on Oliver for everything?

'What do you say, Nora?' Oliver asked. 'Are you happy? You'll love Templemore, and I'm sure that my family will love you.'

Nora looked into Oliver's earnest brown eyes and forgot her doubts. Despite her shock, she was prepared to go anywhere, so long as she was beside her new husband. She knew that she would love him forever and felt sure that he would love her back just as much.

'I *am* happy,' Nora said. 'And I'm sure that we will have a wonderful life in Templemore. I can't wait to get to know your family.'

'You won't be far from your parents in Thurles,' Oliver reminded her. 'They're bound to come round soon, when they get to know me. Especially when they see that I'm well able to provide for you and the kids.'

His powers of persuasion did the trick and soon she was looking forward to the move, even privately allowing herself a little excitement at the thought of a new baby – preferably a boy, and preferably one that resembled Oliver. When she shut her eyes and imagined Oliver in the sunshine of Templemore with their child on his knee, smiling that gentle smile of his, it seemed obvious that Ireland was the place where their happiness would really begin to bear fruit. But the reality of her new life was to leave Nora disillusioned forever.

3

Back to Tipperary

Back home in Tipperary the newly-weds found that nothing had changed and that the narrowness of the small-town mentality and the sniping gossip continued, regardless of the drama and tragedy that had just played out on the world stage. Even Oliver had underestimated how much he valued his city lifestyle and, although his dream of working in the family business had prompted the return to Templemore, it was soon clear to his family and friends that he was likely to become increasingly restless with this quiet, uneventful life. Gradually, inevitably almost, the boredom of his lifestyle began to drive him to the pub.

At a time when most girls from rural backgrounds went straight from school to work for wealthy families or in local shops, Nora was an unusually well-educated and experienced young woman and as soon as she arrived in Templemore she felt the difference between herself and the women around her. There was no companionship to fill the void left by the loss of her three Manchester friends and Oliver's sisters seemed quite disinterested in getting to know their new sister-in-law. Her own sisters had been warned by their parents to keep their distance from Nora and her new family since the Langleys disapproved of the McManuses. She felt trapped at home with nothing to do but to keep house for her husband, even though this was the accepted lifestyle for most women whose husbands could afford to support them – and many whose husbands could not. Oliver may have been bored and restless at work, but at least he found solace in the social life of the pub. Nora was quite simply desperately homesick and lonely twenty-four hours a day.

The situation was made worse by her parents' continuing disapproval of Oliver and their lack of support. The Langleys quickly accepted that marriage within the Catholic Church had trapped their daughter in this union for life and grudgingly they agreed to meet Oliver. But privately they continued to shake their heads sadly at the life Nora had chosen. How could she have settled for a modest terraced house in a small town, when she could have been the mistress of a comfortable farmhouse near their own home? With her many accomplishments and fine looks (which she always made the most of by wearing the latest fashions) she had surely thrown herself away on a man who was unworthy of her. For her part, Nora was very distressed by the rift with her parents. She hoped that it might heal with the passing of time and that she could gradually nurture a good relationship between the Langleys and Oliver, but nothing she did seemed to work. Tom and Ellen Langley were determined to dislike their new son-in-law and Oliver, being proud, did very little to try and win them over.

*

The street where the young couple lived was very ordinary and simple, just like thousands of such streets in small towns all over Ireland. The houses were in terraces of only four, ensuring easy access to the rear for coal and turf or anything else bulky that could not be brought in the front entrance. Each of the houses had a front garden with a path in the middle that led to the door and to either side of the path were tidy lawns and neatly trimmed hedges marking the boundaries. Most of the gardens also had one carefully maintained circular flower bed set into a stretch of the front lawn. Although their homes were modest, the householders took a great deal of pride in them and invested a lot of time and effort in their upkeep. Nobody wanted to have the only untidy, scruffy house in the row.

In the small back garden behind Nora and Oliver's house grew a great lilac bush that bloomed in early summer, perfuming the whole street with the heady, sweet fragrance wafting from its plumes of purple flowers and attracting masses of happy, buzzing bees in search of its nectar. Aside from the lilac there was just enough room in the garden for a shed and a home-made swing fashioned from a piece of rope and the seat of an old kitchen chair. This is where the children would play, when they came along. For now, the neighbours' children were happy to oblige. There was also a shelter where coal and turf were kept dry in the winter. Nora lamented the fact that she had no room to grow potatoes, onions and turnips to supplement the family diet. When she was growing up in Ballycurran everyone had had the space for at least a few vegetables, and sometimes some chickens as well. Oliver assured her that he would be more than able to provide for her and the family that they would soon have, but the lack of her own plot still made Nora a little sad and homesick.

A great sense of camaraderie flourished amongst the women on the street and, after the day's housework was done and the families had been fed and washed, they would all come out of their houses and stand at their gates to have a gossip with whoever was passing by. Sometimes they would spend an entire evening sitting on their windowsills and chatting from one house to another, this being a pleasant way to socialise while they kept an eye on the children as they played outside.

The two Miss Gleesons had no children to watch, since they were unmarried sisters who lived together and had no other family to speak of, but more often than not they could be found sitting on their doorstep or leaning over their gate, while offering a running commentary on the neighbour women as they went about their business. 'Good evening,' they would say politely, smiling broadly at any woman who walked by. But as soon as the woman in question was out of earshot the gloves were off and they would set to: 'Do you see that one? Well now, the trouble she caused her parents and the drinking she does, wouldn't you think butter wouldn't melt in her mouth when you see her walking with her head in the air? Who does she think she is?'

Since money was tight for many of the women a visit to a professional hairdresser was out of the question. Most days they dressed their hair themselves and would put it up out of the way in a simple bun, or perhaps plaited and coiled on the back of their heads. From time to time, however, they did each other's hair and this was always a welcome opportunity for socialising and gossip. The world could be put to rights over the scissors. For special occasions there was the careful use of pipe-cleaners that, in capable hands, could be used to make soft curls or ringlets. Although it was recognised that the pipe-cleaners made the night's sleep fairly uncomfortable, it was considered worth it for the pretty effect it gave the next day.

Nora was timid and felt herself separate right from the start, but her new neighbours were fascinated by her difference and keen to get to know her. They were soon knocking at the door offering to dress her thick brown hair, in the hope that the intimacy of the hairdressing session would encourage her to tell stories about her life in England. Although she was polite she did not find it easy to make friends and, aside from a couple of women with whom she drank tea most days, she never became close to the other women on the street.

Her neighbours might chatter amongst themselves about her 'standoffishness', but they privately admired her for her bravery in striking out on her own to foreign parts and trapping a rather dashing husband there. Some of them would tease her, telling her that she had lost her soft Thurles accent and picked up a bit of an English twang, but they were desperate for her tales of Manchester streets and dance halls. Many of them had barely left Templemore in the whole of their lives and England seemed to them a far away, rather exotic, destination. Some had longed to go and work there themselves –or even America or Canada – but they had not had the fare to go, or had found themselves with small children or elderly parents to take care of. Time had passed and the opportunity and courage to leave had slipped away. None would admit it, but at least a handful must have felt slightly inferior to their pretty, shy, new neighbour.

And then there was the womanising husband, of course. It was worth doing Nora's hair for any titbits that might be gleaned (over the pipe-cleaners) on the subject of Oliver. Since there was not much in the way of a social life to provide topics of conversation (if you discounted the odd hurling match on a Sunday afternoon), the merest whiff of scandal would keep everyone occupied for weeks. Oliver's reputation had been known to the women of Templemore for many moons before Nora came on the scene – the truth was that most of the young women would gladly have walked in her shoes. The fact that their mothers had warned them off Oliver in the past only served to add to his allure. 'Everyone' knew that several of the married women in town were rumoured to have had children by him, fathered (people said) when he was just a teenager (although of course nothing could be proven). But the women of Templemore still basked in the 'glad eye' he invariably gave the fairer sex, even although he was now 'spoken for'. They sniffed excitement in him and envied Nora the zest her dangerous husband brought to her dull life.

*

Babies were always big news in the street and (possibly due to the fascination of the philandering Oliver) the women watched Nora particularly keenly for any change in her shape. Before long their curiosity was rewarded. After just a few months of marriage Nora was delighted to learn that she was expecting her first child and that the dream that had kept her going since Oliver had first produced the boat tickets was finally to become a reality. However she was quite taken aback by her neighbours' direct questions about her pregnancy and the symptoms that accompanied it. Most of the local women knew everything there was to know about each other and almost any topic was considered appropriate for conversation, so long as there was no man within earshot. In part this was because the houses were so close together that there was no possibility of keeping a secret. A row between a married couple might just as well have been conducted in the middle of the road for all the privacy the four walls of their home offered.

Nora hoped that her pregnancy and the birth of their first child would bring her closer to Oliver again. She had no idea yet that his attention had already strayed to other women, but she was a lonely young wife and she longed for the happy intimacy of their first days together in Manchester. Instead, as Nora bloomed, her body grew large and cumbersome and Oliver seemed not to want to even acknowledge her pregnancy.

Just like her neighbours Nora arranged to have her baby at home in her own bed, assisted by a local woman who was the designated midwife. But Nora set her own independent pattern and each of her six babies would appear in the world in the same way – with a minimum of help and no fuss at all. She would never send for the midwife until very close to the end and, by the time the birth woman had arrived, Nora had always got the fire going with a few pots on the boil to sterilise any instruments. She would also have laid out some nice white towels and, of course, some baby clothes, with a white length of cotton to put around the baby's tummy to keep the belly button from popping out. She never made a sound while giving birth: when the pains worsened she simply pulled the bed sheet over her head and pushed as hard as she could to bring the baby into the world.

This first child was an adorable little boy. Nora named him Oliver, after his father, but everyone called him Ollie. Unfortunately his name was almost all that his father gave Ollie. Nora longed for her husband to take an interest in his son and hoped he would be proud to have an heir, but most of the time he just referred to the baby as 'it'. If the baby was quiet, all was well and Oliver might even give his son a cuddle, but as soon as the cries started the infant was promptly thrust back to Nora.

'I'm off out,' he would remark as he put on his hat and jacket and opened the door to leave. 'Please God it will have stopped its bawling by the time I get back. Make sure it's gone to bed by then, won't you?' And then he would leave, without so much as a backward glance.

Gradually Nora realised that her dreams of how grand and happy her marriage would be were nothing more than that – dreams. After only a year or so of marriage Oliver and Nora were fighting all too regularly, mostly about work and not having enough money to pay for the essentials to feed a family and keep house. But there was worse to come. Nothing could have prepared Nora for the violence. Oliver had come from a family that weren't afraid to strike out and he soon turned the habits he had learned in his childhood home against his young wife. There were times when she was embarrassed to walk down the street in Templemore because she knew that everyone must have heard the roars and shouts emanating from their terraced house the night before. And then there were the bruises, all too visible on her delicate, pale skin. Sometimes she stayed indoors for days until the bruises and the associated gossip, especially from the Gleeson sisters, had subsided.

There were many nights when Nora could not get to sleep. She would stay awake, waiting for Oliver to return from a night of drinking and playing cards with his friends. She lay there, rigid with fear, knowing that at that very moment he was turning the charm on for his friends, singing and acting the fool to make them laugh with stories and impersonations of the locals, and the pranks he'd played on unsuspecting strangers. But she knew that the minute he walked through the door of his own home it would be a different face he showed her. A sneering, angry face that was barely recognisable as that of the man she had married just a few years before. Often she would pretend to be asleep when he stumbled drunkenly in, hoping that he would fall into bed and pass out peacefully. But on at least some of those awful nights Oliver would insist on his 'marital rights'. It was inevitable that Nora would soon be pregnant with another MacManus baby.

*

Nora's family grew quickly. Soon she was the mother of three small children – Ollie, Betty and Johnny – all close in age. As the children grew older they, too, suffered from their father's drunkenness and selfish behaviour. What with the cooking and cleaning and caring for them all, Nora was exhausted. And there was no respite because she never went out. Oliver, on the other hand, was always out. Worse still, when he returned in the early hours of the morning, he seemed to delight in waking the whole family to ask them what they had done all day – this from a man who never checked (while sober) to see if his children were well, or wondered where they got their clothes or noticed if they were hungry.

His attitude infuriated and shocked Nora. Over and over again she would plead for his help, but it was never forthcoming. The promises he had made during his courtship seemed like dry dust now. She came to realise that she was raising the children on her own, as Oliver rarely provided enough money to care for them and seemed to have no interest in their welfare. And so, gradually, inevitably, she also stopped pleading for his help.

The McManus family were not remotely interested in Nora's plight – perhaps they felt they had enough problems of their own. Possibly some of them imagined that she thought herself better than they (being the daughter of a schoolmaster and having worked in Manchester) and therefore not deserving of or needing their help.

Whatever it was, there was no one that Nora could lean on. Finally she admitted to herself that her parents had been right all along: she would have been better off in a loveless marriage. However, she swore that she would never ever admit this to them. That would be the final humiliation.

4

Apparitions in Templemore

During those years in which Nora's family was slowly increasing in size, Ireland struggled to achieve her independence. The Irish police force, the Royal Irish Constabulary, was targeted by the Irish Republican Brotherhood and the Irish Republican Army and their barracks were frequently attacked. The British found it increasingly difficult to recruit decent officers to the RIC and in 1920 they responded to the emergency by sending over the notorious 'Black and Tans', temporary constables whose task was to subdue the insurgents by fair means or foul.

Far from being a peacekeeping force, these were mostly soldiers whose experiences in the trenches of France had brutalised them and they seemed to positively enjoy opportunities to terrorise the communities into which they had been sent. There was a song about the British prime minister and his Chief Secretary for Ireland that did the rounds: 'Said Lloyd George to Macpherson, I'll give you the sack / For to govern Ireland you have not the knack / I'll send over Greenwood, a much stronger man / And he'll do my work with the bold Black and Tan.'

They came from every sort of background and, after passing only an elementary literacy test, they were accepted with few questions about their characters or suitability for police duties. In short, they were a terrible bunch of brigands and rogues who quickly raised the hackles of the townspeople of Templemore with their brutality, carelessness and lack of respect. Several young local men were killed by these vicious intruders and their friends were forced to face the scorn and laughter of the Black and Tans when they scurried back to retrieve their mangled remains. Anger peaked and the District Inspector was shot on the street in broad daylight, killed by a bullet that entered his body through the back of his neck. The locals stopped short of rejoicing openly. Tensions were high and people were nervous, but it was clear that even more shocking events might be expected.

*

Mr Duane was the local newsagent and he lived above his shop, five minutes from the police barracks. His was a prosperous small business because it was considered hugely important, even in a small town in rural Ireland, to have a good command of world affairs. Mr Duane and his family, just like the rest of Templemore's inhabitants, had been suffering from the stress of recent events. He and his neighbours lay awake at night and worried throughout the daylight hours about what was to become of them all. Mr Duane was simply trying to keep his head down and his small business above water. He did not want to get into trouble with the hated authorities, but nor did he want to be seen to be collaborating with them. He just wished that the whole sorry mess would come to an end so that he could continue with his business of supplying the townspeople with newspapers and magazines and passing the time of day pleasantly over the counter. But soon Mr Duane's ordinary, simple home would be renowned the length and breadth of Ireland.

A few miles outside Templemore is a mountain known as the Devil's Bit, which towers over the little townland of Curraheen. James Welsh, a seventeen-year-old farm labourer, hailed from this very spot. The Devil's Bit is a beautiful mountain that dominates the landscape in this part of the Irish midlands but at that time the little townland at its feet was home to some of the greatest poverty in the region. It was inhabited by small farmers and labourers who lived in homes that were barely more than huts, built from clods of earth, roofed with thatch and furnished with odds and ends that other people had thrown away. It was from such a poor family that James Welsh came.

Welsh might have been just a labourer, but he was also a dreamy youth who was fascinated by the spiritual side of life. Apparently he had longed to become a priest until his health had prevented him from studying, after which Mr Duane's sister had employed him to work on her farm, a practical job for which he was particularly ill-suited. James was a thin, sensitive, intelligent boy who had never seemed completely at ease in the world and the newsagent, having been struck by the lad when he met him on his sister's farm, had befriended him, feeling a little sorry for the intelligent young man who had been forced by circumstances to make a living working with his hands. Mr Duane set aside old newspapers and magazines for him because he knew that James could not afford to buy books. He knew that James was an unusual character but he was not prepared for what would happen on the day of the District Inspector's funeral.

James was visiting the Duanes on the day and, as the funeral cortège passed, he turned to Mr Duane and remarked, 'It is time to give my message to the world and you must be the one to help me.' Mr Duane had no idea what James was talking about but he could see from the fire in the boy's eyes that it was important. He later told his friends that he had felt chilled to the bone when James spoke those strange words.

'The Blessed Virgin appeared to me above at the Devil's Bit,' James said, his deep eyes full of conviction and his knuckles white as he clutched Mr Duane's forearm. 'I saw her with my own two eyes, as beautiful as could be. She told me how upset she is about the sinful happenings in Ireland and she asked me to let the people know that she is here for them, to listen to their prayers and to intercede on their behalf.'

Mr Duane stared silently at James as he continued, 'She told me to scrape a small hole in the earthen floor of my house. No sooner had I done so, than the hole filled with water that seemed to come from nowhere. Within moments, it was a clear, running spring, bubbling up from the ground. I fell onto my knees and started to pray and, as I did, the statue started to bleed and the air filled with the scent of roses! I swear to you, Mr Duane, all of this happened exactly as I am telling you.'

To Mr Duane's astonishment James rooted around in his bag and handed him a small plaster statue of the Virgin Mary. There were some rust-coloured marks on it that Welsh identified as dried blood. The statue appeared just as ordinary as the plaster images that adorned most Catholic homes but, because of the reverence with which James held it, Mr Duane accepted it in the same spirit. He looked at the smears on the figurine's face. They *did* look like blood.

'I need you to keep this in your house for me,' James said. 'You'll see, miracles are going to happen in Templemore! The death of the District Inspector was the first sign and this is the second!'

The next day, while the town still buzzed with reports of the funeral, Welsh had another vision. According to him the Blessed Virgin had appeared again and claimed that, because of her intervention, the Black and Tans had been brought under control in Templemore and the whole town saved from destruction. This information was obviously greeted with great excitement by Templemore's inhabitants who were desperate for any ray of hope in these difficult times.

'It's time,' Welsh said to his friend Mr Duane. 'We need to tell people what has been happening in Templemore so that they can pray for their own souls and for the future of Ireland.'

Together they carried a small table from the house into the yard behind the newsagent's shop and laid a white linen cloth on it. They placed three statues of the Blessed Virgin Mary on the cloth. From the face of each statue a dark, shiny trickle of blood ran down onto the white cloth. Soon the crowds began to gather in the town as news spread of the strange happenings. Everyone came out to see what the excitement was all about and the policemen kept a watchful eye on the proceedings, mindful that in the highly charged atmosphere of the day even a religious gathering could quickly descend into chaos and violence. There was a great commotion when a wild-eyed, hysterical man came down the main street dancing and leaping in the air. He was laughing and shouting out his praise and thanks to God.

'Look at me!' he shouted. 'I'm healed. I'm healed!'

The people gathered around. They all knew Liam. For as long as they could remember he had been dragging his twisted legs about the streets of Templemore with the aid of crutches. But here he was, before a laughing, weeping, hysterical, praying crowd, his body as normal as could be and his face alight with joy and religious fervour. There was no sign of any disability at all. They were told that he had been out to Welsh's house on the Devil's Bit and had drunk the water from the well inside the home, a well that had suddenly appeared where no well had ever been before. He had gone straight down the mountain and thrown the crutches away. Templemore was witnessing its first miracle. The news spread like wildfire. Some believed that it was really an intercession of the Blessed Virgin. Others said that it was the devil's work. There were those who dismissed it as phantasy invented by their neighbours. Whatever you thought on the day Liam threw away his crutches, it was surely the most positive thing that had happened for a long time in a world dominated by the dark shadows of the Black and Tans.

When the local newspaper was published the following morning, it told the story of the bleeding statues, the holy well and the straightened cripple. Then, as if on a rising tide, the news spread throughout Ireland and the story was bringing hope and wonder to homes that had known only illness and infirmity. A steady trickle of pilgrims became a noisy river as people set out to travel to Templemore with the idea of receiving a miracle of their own, hoping that whatever ailed them could be repaired.

*

Nora's dream was that the Blessed Virgin's miraculous powers might save her marriage from misery. By this time she had heard the rumours of Oliver's womanising and his bastard offspring and she dared to hope that her prayers might stop him drinking and behaving as he did. In desperation she visited Duane's place with a whispered prayer on her lips and saw for herself the bleeding statues. Daringly she reached out and touched the trickles of blood on the white linen tablecloth and, for a day or two afterwards, she allowed herself to hope that something would happen, that there would be a change for the better.

Nora's prayers were in vain. Oliver had always been attracted to danger and as soon as the insurgent attacks on the Black and Tans started up he was drawn to the thick of it. Excitement was life's blood to him and the action in and around Templemore reminded him of his wartime activities. Like his comrades he also felt deeply disillusioned. He and many thousands of Irishmen had fought for the British army in good faith and made considerable sacrifices – and still they were being treated like dogs in their own country. His activities had a negative impact on his home life, however, since he thought that the rebel action was much more important than putting food on the table for his children. If there was freedom for Ireland, he reasoned, the food would naturally follow. Life had previously been difficult for Nora and her offspring but with Oliver's new heroism things were about to become much worse.

Before long the Black and Tans had added Oliver's name to their list of activists and he was regularly forced to take shelter in a safe house when local intelligence tipped the insurgents off that the 'Tans' were on the move. A Mrs Green kindly offered Oliver a safe haven whenever he needed it and, because she lived close to Templemore, it was fairly easy to dodge down his personal rabbit hole whenever the alarm went up. Since Oliver spent a good deal of time hiding under her bed, it was fortunate that she was a respectable, middle-aged woman into whose bedroom the Black and Tans would never think to venture in search of their quarry. There was, however, a price to pay in return for Mrs Green's hospitality. When Oliver came out from under Mrs Green's bed, he was expected to hop under the sheets with the older woman and offer her his services as a lover. As she was still an attractive lady, if a little older than his usual amours, Oliver was only too happy to oblige.

Mrs Green (a woman well into her forties) was surprised to suddenly find herself pregnant, long after she had assumed her childbearing days were over. And it was hardly surprising that many a wagging tongue wondered if Mr Green, a much older man, still had it in him to get his wife in the family way. At which point Oliver's name was thrown into the mix, since it was fairly common knowledge that he had often sought 'refuge' in her home. Naturally ribald remarks as to the exact nature of this 'refuge' were soon doing the rounds. But, since there was no actual proof of paternity and it was probably easier and less embarrassing for Mr Green to rear the baby as his own than to publicly admit his wife had been deceiving him, it seemed that Oliver had probably got away with it again. The gossip about Oliver and Mrs Green even reached Nora's ears but she dismissed it as being irrelevant to her. At that point she was more concerned that Oliver might be killed or sent to prison. Then she would have nobody to support her at all.

*

The Irish signed a peace treaty with the government of Great Britain in December 1921 and the Black and Tans left Ireland for good. The Civil War would continue to disrupt the normal life of Templemore but, fortunately for Nora, Oliver had tired of playing soldiers and returned to work at the cobbler's. He also returned to Nora's bed.

In May 1923, a month after Nora and Oliver's fourth wedding anniversary, the Civil War petered out into the ceasefire and most ordinary Irish citizens felt nothing more than quiet relief that the situation seemed to be resolved. Although life was still far from perfect for most families, at least there was no longer the daily worry that a loved one might be killed or taken away to prison. In Templemore even the excitement over the bleeding statues faded quite quickly. Now the rumour was that from the very start the story had been a distraction, allowing the IRA time to move to safe houses when the Tans had been closing in on them. Whatever the case, the deep wounds that had ruptured communities and caused suspicion to flourish between brothers and among friends would not heal quickly.

Nora's three children grew bigger and Oliver settled back into work with his father and brothers, soling shoes and putting studs on the soles of Templemore's boots so that they would last longer. The town rang to the sound of these studded boots since all the men wore them. In those days everyone made the most of what they had, even people who were better off than Nora and Oliver. And there were families that were poorer too, families that could not afford a visit to the cobbler at all. These people soled their own shoes. Almost every house kept a wooden butter box in which they stored small household items such as a screwdriver, a few nails, an awl and a last, screws, pieces of leather, a folding timber ruler and everything they needed to carry out daily repairs on their shoes. Hemp was used to sew the soles, the string pulled through a block of wax to make it waterproof. There was no question of simply replacing shoes if there was any way in which they could be fixed.

Oliver himself wore a pair of studded boots, although admittedly the furthest he ever walked was to the local pub after work. Waiting for his return after a night's drinking and playing cards with his friends was still a nightmare for Nora. She gave in to all his demands and yet he never seemed to notice how much she relinquished for him. Even on the nights when he did come home soon after work, he often entertained his friends by singing loudly in the small parlour downstairs as the children tried to sleep. But worse were the nights when he stayed in the pub until late and came home with 'the drink in him'. On those nights Nora knew that a row would start, no matter how hard she tried to placate him. Mostly she tried to pretend she was asleep when she heard the key in the lock, hoping the storm would pass, but when he was drunk he often forgot his keys and then the whole neighbourhood would hear him pounding on the door to summon her downstairs. The children were generally sound asleep when they were awoken by the banging.

'Let me in, woman,' Oliver would shout. 'Get yourself out of bed and come downstairs and take care of your husband or I'll come up there and get you out myself.'

When Nora went down he would blame her for not having stayed awake so as to let him in and he would demand that she prepare him something to eat although, as Oliver himself had drunk the family's money for the week, the larder was often empty.

The children shook in their beds at the thought of their father coming up the stairs. Nora would try and restrain him from going up to the children's rooms but when he had the drink in him nothing could stop him from shouting and creating a rumpus. His intention was to 'put the fear of God on' the whole household and let them know that he was the boss and the lord and master. As if any of them could ever forget it. In this state Oliver did not care about how much he hurt or frightened his children. He was convinced it was important for them to respect his authority. But they dreaded the sound of him coming into the room where they were supposed to be sleeping. The minute his figure loomed in the doorway they knew that a terrible inquisition would begin and they covered their ears, trying hard not to hear him shouting and stamping his feet on the wooden floor.

'What did you do all day?' he would shout. 'What did you get up to? What were you doing all day long? What the hell goes on in this house when I am not here? Why am I not respected as a father should be? Is it your mother, telling you lies about me again? Where are your manners, you shower of ungrateful little wretches?'

Oliver would demand that the whole family get out of their beds to stand by the wall and wait for his orders. Despite the fact that it was the middle of the night, he would ask all three of the children, who were still very small, to carry out chores around the house and then chastise them if they did not perform them adequately. He did not know whether or not they had gone to bed hungry and he did not really care. Treated as badly as they were, it was not surprising that the children often felt unloved and unwanted by their father. But what really broke Nora's heart was the sound of the three of them crying when he turned on her, shouting at her that she was a whore when she made herself look nice and a slattern when she did not.

She tried so hard to protect them. Every night, before the children went to bed, she would gather them together and plead, 'Don't make a sound when Daddy comes in.

Just do what he says and don't answer him back. If you are all very good and very quiet he will be better in the morning and everything will be alright again.' Nora knew she had no control over Oliver's behaviour. Women of her generation promised to honour and obey at the altar and that was that, they had no authority in their own homes if their husbands chose to ignore them.

There was a softer side to Oliver that he occasionally allowed his family to see when he was sober. He even seemed to be fond of them sometimes, in his own distant way. He did not give them gifts or pocket money, because there was no money, but he would recite poems and sing songs with them. He would pick them up and sit them on his knee, smooth their hair and tell them that they were beautiful. As a result of his abilities as a raconteur, they knew all the old Irish riddles and funny stories and they would remember them for the rest of their lives.

Their mother was terrified of thunder and lightning, always rushing to hide under the stairs when a storm came, and so Oliver was at pains to banish that fear from his children's lives. He taught them not to be afraid of the storm, reassuring them that it could not harm them. Whenever there were loud claps of thunder he would stand the children up on the kitchen table so that they could see out the window. 'Go on,' he would say. 'Look out the window at the rain. See the lightning? There's nothing to be scared of! No McManus has ever let a little lightning upset him. It's just God's way of reminding us that he's still there.' The children soon learned to laugh at their mammy's reaction to the storm.

These good days were few and far between. Soon Oliver would be off getting drunk again and have another row with Nora. And then, then the smallest thing would set him off on a rampage around the house, calling the three of them wicked and threatening them with the belt from his waist. He did not always use it but he often took it off to scold the children or removed his shoe to hit. When the 'morning after' finally arrived, it would not just be Oliver who rose with a headache. The children, too, would be nursing bruises and sore heads but would never admit outside their home how they had come by their injuries. The rare nights when the little dictator came home and simply went to sleep in his own bed were the greatest of blessings.

5

Templemore 'doings' and a new arrival

Hunting for rabbits was a common occupation for the townspeople, many of whom could not afford to buy meat very often and relied on their own efforts to fill the pot and give their children something other than the boiled bacon and cabbage that featured so prominently on the menu. There were families who swore that they had been kept alive all winter by the efforts of their dog and a good dog was a very prized possession indeed.

Oliver's favourite brother was Victor, who was nearest him in age and also worked at the shoemaking. Victor was a keen hunter and kept a large number of hounds. Whenever he was not at work he was out in the fields and farms around Templemore, returning with the rabbits strung on a stick by the simple method of cutting a hole in one hind leg and threading the other one through. He hunted rabbits less out of necessity than for sport, but the resulting meat was still very warmly received by family and friends.

Victor and his trusty hound would go out at night armed with a lamp fashioned from an old battery attached to a bulb and would meet up with a group of his hunting mates on the outskirts of town. Catching rabbits was a refined skill that was passed from father to son. The men knew how to enter fields with the wind in their faces rather than at their backs to ensure that their scent was carried away from them and not straight to the rabbits, which would scurry into their burrows at the first hint of the hunters' presence. It was important to avoid the little paths where the rabbits habitually passed in order to avoid leaving their scent on them, but the most frequently used tracks were the ideal spots to set up rabbit snares. These the men made with a stick and a loop of wire that would tighten around the animal's head when it was caught and that would not release it, regardless of how hard it struggled to get free. The snares would do their work during the hours of darkness and at daybreak the men would go and collect their prey. Their families were very happy on those days and so were the dogs, which were kept lean so as not to suppress their hunting instincts.

Back at the house the women skinned the animals and threw intestines, heads and legs to the excited hounds, which fell upon them hungrily. They made delicious, rich rabbit stew from the meat, flavoured with onions and herbs and served with potatoes, and then they set the skins aside to be treated and turned into hats and gloves. The bones were boiled to make stock that would give a bit of flavour and substance to vegetable soup on the following day. On the days when the catch was very good, the rabbit stew that could not be eaten straight away was bottled and set aside in the larder for those times when there was nothing else. Nothing was wasted and there was no thought of throwing even a scrap away.

Of course Oliver was far too elegant to consider going hunting himself, so the availability of rabbit meat in Nora's kitchen depended on Victor's hunting success and his whim. Whenever Victor presented Oliver with something for the pot he would bring it home, flinging the dead animal on the table for Nora to clean and skin.

'There,' he would say. 'Don't say I never do anything for this family.'

Nora would not respond but would silently take the rabbit away and prepare it to cook with whatever few vegetables and potatoes she had to hand. Her children were thin and pale and she felt that they needed all the meat they could get.

*

In those days most people found their entertainment at home, whether the times were peaceful or tumultuous. In the evenings friends gathered together to chat for hours in their local 'rambling house'. Every neighbourhood, urban or rural, had its rambling house where all the news and views were exchanged and where the local gossip grew to such dimensions that it was often difficult to identify the original story at the heart of an embellished one. In the course of just one night the topics of conversation could range from ghost stories to history lessons, to news of the latest death in the area, sicknesses that were affecting the local population, and any other item of interest. The rambling house was popularly known as the 'news room' because whenever there was any news to be had it would be heard there first.

Many of the speakers at the rambling houses had little formal education and some could not even read and write, relying on someone else to read aloud for them from the newspaper. But although they travelled rarely, if ever, beyond the confines of their own county, everyone shared a fascination with world affairs and a desire to be well-informed. The lucky few had a 'wet and dry' battery-operated radio with acid that needed to be changed periodically, because without fresh acid there would be no sound. Mothers took the radio to be charged every week and cautioned children not to touch it for fear of acid burns. The children regarded the radio with a kind of awe. As more families acquired radios they began to hear the news of the world more directly and to realise how small their corner of it was. As well as listening to the radio, anyone who could afford it would be sure to buy newspaper at least once a week to keep up with the times. This practice was a matter of personal pride, since it ensured that they could hold their own in a rambling house debate.

When current events had been exhausted at the 'news room', the speakers would revisit stories of days gone by. Men exchanged tales of army life in the war and of the exploits of the local IRA men. Some of those present would have been on the run from the Black and Tans just a few short years before and the exact location of safe houses always stimulated a lively discussion. Life was still uncertain in the new Irish republic and there was certainly plenty to debate of an evening. Oliver was, of course, a frequent visitor and a lively speaker at his own local 'news room'.

When the big screen came to town it was a great occasion for one and all. In the years before the 'movies' one of the few forms of entertainment available to young single women had been a visit to the local fortune-teller to hear that they would meet a nice man and marry, have a big family and live happily ever after. The 'pictures' were definitely better value for money, and everyone agreed that their arrival proved Templemore was no longer just a small town but a place to be reckoned with. What was more, now that the big world lay at their doorstep life was bound to be more exciting. If the priests and older people in the town issued dire warnings about the effect of frequent picture-going on the morals of Templemore's youngsters, the young people themselves paid not a blind bit of notice. As Templemore became more sophisticated (in the eyes of its residents, at least), the picture house became one of 'the' places to be seen.

The arrival of the movies scarcely touched Nora's life. She had loved going to the pictures in Manchester when she and Oliver had been courting and had often compared her lover very favourably to the handsome actors whom she had seen on the screen. Now, in common with many of her female neighbours, there was barely enough money to pay for the necessities of life, never mind cinema tickets. The women did what they knew best, keeping their homes together and their children fed in the face of all the difficulties that confronted them. Even though most Irishwomen had so little and were poor, they maintained their sense of pride. Who wanted to complain to their family and friends? The women all did their best to hold their heads high and make the most of their lives.

As Nora's horizons closed in on her, the memory of that other life in Manchester seemed like a distant, sad dream. She became increasingly anxious and depressed, losing interest in anything beyond her monotonous daily routine and the constant drudgery of keeping the house clean and the children fed and clothed on the scraps that were left from Oliver's salary after his forays to local pubs and rambling houses. She found little time for, or interest in, her appearance and her delicate good looks began to fade as a result of the constant stress of having to provide for her children with little or nothing. As well as being physically exhausted from having children so close together, she was still being beaten regularly by her husband. Most shamefully, she knew that in spite of the fact that she kept her predicament to herself, her family's plight provided plenty of material for the neighbourhood gossips. 'Is he good enough for her?' they would ask each other. Or, 'Is she suitable for him?' They made it all too clear that they knew Oliver did not provide properly for his wife and three children.

Other people's marriages and financial woes were always a popular topic for gossips such as the Misses Gleeson. They set particular store by the possession of land. Marriage to a man with land, even if he was no longer young, was not handsome and was a dour fellow, was seen as the ideal arrangement for any young woman. The land was always there and those who owned it could survive the hard times and would always have something of value to pass on to their children. As for love, popular wisdom maintained that it could grow where there was prosperity but withered in the face of hunger. Women with land could grow their own fresh vegetables, raise a calf and have a cow for the milk. They could keep some pigs and kill one every now and then for the family. 'Lucky is the girl who marries a man with land,' was the women's view. Nora's parents rarely visited her now, but whenever she heard this kind of chatter from her neighbours she was haunted by thoughts of the rich old farmer they had picked out for her.

*

Nora's fourth child was due in September 1926. It was a hot summer that year and carrying the baby was very tiring for her, especially because she had three boisterous older children to care for. The children were happy about the summer heat – they could take off their boots and go barefoot and they could play out of doors on those long, balmy summer evenings. But for a heavily pregnant young mother with an unsupportive husband and a family that had turned its collective back on her, it was a very difficult time indeed.

The due date came and went and Nora grew anxious, but after three days the baby girl was born at home in Nora's bedroom. Following the pattern she had already set with the other births, Nora called the midwife late and the woman arrived just in time to see Kitty making her way into the world. Just in time, in fact, to shout, 'It's a baby girl, about eight pounds in weight!'

The birth woman checked all her vital signs. 'She's a good, healthy baby, Mrs McManus. What will you name her?'

Nora paused for a moment. Then, 'Kathleen,' she said. 'But I will shorten it to 'Kitty'. It's a pretty name for a pretty girl.'

'Kitty it is.'

The midwife wrapped the baby in a soft woollen blanket and handed her to her mother. Exhausted, Nora put the infant to her breast and closed her eyes to relax for a moment before the other three children stormed in, clamouring to see their new baby sister and to cover her in kisses.

At that moment, the world had been given a new, astonishing person: a little girl who would climb every mountain in her path, regardless of how high it was, and who would never let anybody stand in the way of her achieving what she felt to be important.

Kitty was christened in the local church on the next Sunday morning and two weeks later Nora was 'churched' in accordance with Roman Catholic law. After giving birth women were considered unclean until they had been churched and thus cleansed of what was seen to be the sinful dirtiness of childbirth. Churching was carried out at the bottom of the church so as not to sully the area near the altar. The women were prayed over and their confessions were heard before they were finally allowed to approach the altar rail and take Communion with the rest of the flock. During that period, even during ordinary Sunday Masses, women would sit on the left of the church while the men sat on the right. The tradition of churching was just one more reminder, if any were needed, that church and society alike considered women and mothers to be very much second-class citizens.

As all the women did, Nora submitted quietly and obediently to this indignity. Because she was a good Catholic wife, she had promised to honour and obey her husband and her church. And this was the very reason that it was so very unlikely Kitty would be her last child.

*

In those years Templemore saw many members of the travelling community pass through. Of course during the 1920s they were known as 'tinkers' rather than 'travellers'. The word 'tinker' is now used pejoratively, but then it was a simple description of a trade, since the tinkers repaired pots and pans at a time when nothing was ever thrown away if it could be reused. They would turn up on the streets of all the little towns like Templemore, do their shopping, sell their bits and pieces and beg whatever they could from the townspeople. Some of the tinkers were also coopers, since they made barrels and buckets that were bound together with hoops. Whatever their skills, they were always very talented salespeople, having studied the art from childhood.

Nora had seen the tinkers on the side of the road near Thurles when she was growing up, but it was only as an adult in Templemore that she began to have close encounters with them, the market town being one of their regular stopping points on their way around Ireland. Everyone knew when the tinkers were coming to town before they reached it, because their colourful, horse-drawn wagons, painted in bright colours with a few scruffy dogs trailing behind, could be seen from a mile or so away. The caravans looked cheerful from a distance but these were the travellers' homes in good weather and bad: freezing in snow and frost and stiflingly hot in the summer.

Once, before Nora had had much to do with them, they set up camp in Templemore near the McManus house. As they arrived, Nora noticed that there were five children in the wagon and that the youngest was probably not older than about one. However, as soon as the horses were tethered, the parents promptly abandoned their five children to take off into town for pickings. Nora became worried that the children had been left with nothing to eat or drink. Emptying her cupboards, she cooked up a big dinner for them, with potatoes and vegetables and even a little bit of meat, and set it all out on plates for them on the street outside the house. The children ate ravenously and asked for more. For three full days Nora fed the unfortunate children, who had no idea where their parents were. On the fourth day they finally came home, reeking of alcohol and having been beaten black and blue.

Ollie, who could not have been more than about five at the time, was jealous of the tinker children.

'Will you make their dinner for me, Mammy?' he begged Nora.

Nora served Ollie the potatoes and vegetables, saying, 'If I had given you that dinner before, you would not have eaten a morsel of it. You only want it now because I made it for somebody else.'

'I wish I lived in a caravan on the side of the road, Mammy,' Ollie sighed. 'I would never have to do what I was told and nobody would ever slap me or scold me or tell me off.'

Nora told Ollie, very shortly, that he did not know how lucky he was to have a nice warm bed to sleep in at night and she reminded him to kneel and say his prayers every night to thank God for all the good things he had.

When Oliver heard that Ollie had been wishing that he was a tinker child, he pulled him onto his knee and told him the story of his father and the fine hunting dog.

'Listen to the story I'm going to tell you about your grandfather Martin's dealings with one of them,' he began, 'and you will soon know why you should stay away from all the tinkers and their ilk.' Years later Ollie would tell the story to Kitty and she never forgot it, because the events of the story had changed her big brother's life.

*

'Despite the fact that the McManuses are well-respected artisans in Templemore, they are never afraid of getting into trouble. A rebellious streak runs through our whole family. Martin, my father and your grandfather, often reminisced about the old days and the many adventures he had before settling down and becoming a serious tradesman. Like your uncle Victor, Dad had been a great man for hunting in his younger years and his dog, which went by the name of Jerry, had been without precedent in the town. Jerry was obedient and clever and very good at bringing home rabbits, pheasants and other game. Everyone who saw Jerry at work agreed that there had never been such a talented creature in the history of the town and that he was probably more intelligent than most human beings, as well as being far faster on his feet. My father was often asked if he would agree to sell Jerry but he always refused, saying that the dog was worth his weight in gold and that he would not give him away for any price.

'Thanks to Jerry, Dad once got himself into trouble so severe that it still affects our family. One day, back when I was just a little boy, a tinker man came to Templemore, having heard of Martin McManus' fine hunting dog. As this man had many mouths to feed and a family in much worse straits than Dad's, he felt justified in stealing the dog for himself. Tinker Brown stole the dog from behind our house late one night, when he thought he would get away with it. In the morning, when Dad awoke, the first thing he did was go to feed Jerry. Usually, the dog jumped eagerly when his master came out in the morning, but today Dad found that the rope that had tied Jerry to the kennel was cut and the dog gone.

'"What the hell has happened here?" Dad shouted in a terrible rage. He rushed out the door and went down the street, asking the neighbours if they had seen anyone taking Jerry from outside his house.

'"I did see Tinker Brown early this morning," one neighbour told him. "He had Jerry behind him on a rope. I noticed that but I assumed that you had sold him the dog, or I would have said something to him."

'"Indeed I did not!" said Dad. "I would never sell my fine hunting dog. That dog puts meat on my family's table and he is the most valuable possession I own in this world. He has been robbed from me but this time they have taken the dog from the wrong man."

'Dad borrowed a bicycle from an accommodating neighbour and set off with all haste to the campsite outside Templemore, only to find that the tinker clan had moved during the night, presumably in hope of getting away with the theft of the dog. Having secured himself the finest hunting dog in Ireland, Tinker Brown was not going to let him go easily. But nor was Dad, and Tinker Brown had not reckoned on his determination to get back his prized hunting dog at whatever cost. Dad caught up with the camp on the move, just a few miles outside Templemore. They had set up on the side of the road and sure enough there was Jerry. Jerry was tied to the wheel of one of the caravans but he leapt to his feet and started to wag his tail and bark happily when he saw his master.

'"Give me back my dog!" Dad shouted, jumping down from his bicycle and throwing it to one side. "Give me back my dog or I swear to you I will make you regret it."

'"I will not," said Tinker Brown. "This is *my* dog now. I found him wandering about the town with no owner in sight. What proof have you that he is yours?"

'With that, Dad rolled up his shirt sleeves and threw himself at Tinker Brown with his fists flying. My father was a big, strong man and Tinker Brown was no match for him. He struck him a blow to the head, knocked him out stone cold, gave him another few thumps for good measure and them calmly untied his dog and took him home.

'But Dad had not realised how badly hurt Tinker Brown was and, with no medical help available, he died there and then on the side of the road to the grief of his whole extended family. And later that day the police called to the house and arrested your grandfather for the murder of Tinker Brown.

'Everyone in Templemore was talking about what had happened. They were all in shock; no one could believe that Martin McManus was capable of murder and the whys and wherefores were discussed for weeks to come. Many of them felt sorry for Tinker Brown's family, as they had been left without a father, but they also found it hard to have a lot of sympathy for the dead man himself. Hadn't he been stealing your grandfather's possessions? Didn't a man have a right to take back what belonged to him? At the same time, murder was murder! They all waited with bated breath to see what the sentence would be.

'The court case was held in the nearby town of Nenagh. When it was heard, many of the townspeople of Templemore went to watch and listen to the proceedings of the case against Martin McManus. Such was the excitement that some even slept rough on the streets so as to be able to sit in a good seat whenever the morning session opened. The courthouse was packed every day, with people turned away in droves because there was not enough space for everyone. The ones who had been turned away sat outside on the streets. Those in Templemore who could not attend eagerly awaited news of the proceedings each evening. Nothing so exciting had ever happened in Templemore before. Tempers ran very high during the two weeks of the trial. Dad had many supporters among his friends and neighbours but the tinker family had its supporters too. Hundreds of tinkers had travelled from all over the country to show their support for one of their own and there were many rowdy scenes outside the courthouse. Dad was attacked every day as he was led from it. There was a heavy police presence outside the courthouse and in the surrounding streets. The local pubs were overflowing with Brown's supporters and other pubs were forced to close because of the outrage that ensued when they refused to serve a tinker. As the crowds grew progressively drunker, emotions ran high and tears flowed as they reminisced about their son, their brother, their friend, who had been cut down in the prime of his life by Martin McManus, all because of a dog.

'After two weeks all the evidence had been heard. Dad's supporters spoke on his behalf and many in the tinker community responded with angry cries when they did not like what they heard. Order was called again and again, and on many occasions people had to be bodily removed from the court because they were causing a disruption. Tinker Brown's mother and sisters were often to be heard shouting obscenities at your grandfather and when that happened they were carried outside and placed on the pavement, not very gently. On some days the chaos grew to the extent that the hearing of evidence had to be cancelled until the following morning.

'Dad testified that he had hit Tinker Brown hard, knocked him to the ground and left him there, but that he had not realised the severity of his injuries and had not expected him to die. When he had taken his stolen dog and left, he had assumed that Tinker Brown would soon be back on his feet and would return to his thieving ways.

'"I am very sorry for what happened," he told the court. "My intention was simply to get back what was mine and not to do any harm to anybody, or deprive any family of a father. I assure you, your Honour and everyone here, that nothing of the sort will ever happen again."

'People knew that my father was a hot-tempered man but the consensus was that he was not capable of murder and that Tinker Brown's death had been a case of manslaughter. Dad could only hope that the court would see things the same way. When he was asked to stand to hear the court's decision, silence reigned in the courtroom for the first time. Sure enough, the sentence was one of manslaughter and it would be suspended. Your grandfather would not have to serve time in jail. As soon as those words were uttered, a great cry arose in court and Tinker Brown's family started to shriek and wail their distress and anger.

'"Unfair," they shouted. "Unfair! He killed our brother! He killed our son! He's a murderer! Take him away!"

'Most of the people in the town felt that Dad had got off quite lightly with a suspended sentence and, while few believed that he really was a cold-blooded murderer, they could not really forget what he had done. Things were never quite the same for our family in Templemore after the untimely death of Tinker Brown. Every now and then the Brown family turns up and seeks out a McManus so as to wreak their revenge on us. Any McManus will do, because the family of Tinker Brown have sworn that they will have their vengeance, even if it takes generations.

'So let that be a lesson to you,' Oliver told Ollie when he had finished. 'Stay well away from the tinkers and let them stay well away from you, because no good can come of having anything to do with their sort. We were made different, and it is better for us all if we stay that way.'

Although Ollie and his siblings had an easier life than most of the tinker children they saw camping around the outskirts of Templemore, things continued to be very difficult. In truth, Oliver had no real cause to think himself better than any tinker father, despite his fighting words.

6

After the gold rush

Templemore had increased its population and there was now an army barracks filled with fine men who delighted the hearts of the local girls. Every

good fun that accompanied them. The men's studded boots, repaired by Oliver's family, made their way across the dance floor and sparks flew as the dances grew wilder and wilder and the girls hid their smiles behind their hands, hoping for a glance from one of those handsome boys.

The dances went on in winter and summer alike. Sometimes thick snow lay on the ground, or it teemed with rain, but whatever the weather the men and women still thronged into the dance halls. Many had travelled for miles on bicycles and by foot to attend a dance. Farmers lucky enough to have tractors drove them into town, packed with young farm labourers out for a night of fun. They parked their tractors or their pony and trap – sometimes just a donkey – down the road and walked the last of the way to the dance hall.

Romance was in the air. The girls giggled and laughed. They were shy at the thought of being seen by the men but not so shy that they wanted to stay at home. Disappointing was the day when they were not allowed to leave the house or had to babysit their younger brothers and sisters. Were they missing the opportunity to meet the love of their lives? There was little the young people would not do to get out in the evening. Nora watched all the commotion from her house and thought bitterly of her own courting days and how disappointed she was in her marriage. She hoped that the pretty young girls she saw with their beaux would have better luck.

The town hall was right in the centre of the town and this was where all the lads and young men gathered in the evenings and at the weekend when they were not at work. There was a fine view of the main street, which was known to be the widest in Ireland and thus a source of considerable local pride. The locals used to refer to it as 'two streets in one,' as it was bifurcated by the town hall. On Saturdays and Sundays the men would stand there to view the girls and women walking up and down the street. During the week men would also gather there when they were looking for a day's work with the builders or the farmers from the rich hinterland around the town. Anyone who wanted a man to work for a day or a week could come to the town hall and collect a fellow willing to provide his labour. Most of the men wanted to work as hard as they could to find a way to support their family.

The cobbler's workshop had seen better days and, although Oliver was heir to the business, in hard times everyone was expected to take a smaller share of the profits. Consequently his weekly pay packet was never enough to fund his taste for drink, fine clothes and cards and still to put food on his family's table. Perhaps he should have been down with the others on weekday mornings trying to supplement his income, but he would not have considered it. He was too proud and, since he was a skilled shoemaker, he would not have dreamt of roughing it on the building sites or the farms – he might get dirty, or damage his fashionably cut clothes.

Despite Oliver's behaviour his parents could see no harm in him at all and were never prepared to listen to Nora's requests for help, as they did not want to contemplate the notion that their beloved son was failing to provide properly for his family. Oliver had a talent for pulling the wool over other people's eyes. Behind her back he told his family many ugly lies about his young wife and blamed her for all their woes. Nora, for her part, never imagined that Oliver would tell them untruths to explain the difficulties at home.

*

For years Oliver had continued to insist that he was still pleased with his decision to move back to Templemore but finally, although he kept his thoughts to himself, he began to question the wisdom of having returned to his home town. The place was just too small and he found living there too restrictive, especially now that he was expected to put food in so many little mouths. And so he decided that he wanted to strike out on his own, leaving the little mouths to fend for themselves. 'Nonnie will take care of them,' he reasoned to himself. 'They will be in safe hands with Nonnie.'

Great-aunt Nonnie lived in the same street as Nora and Oliver. She and her sister Mary had left for America in the 1870s at a time when many in Ireland still did not have enough to eat, in spite of the fact that the terrible Famine years of 1845 to 1852 were behind them. The choice was stark: they could emigrate or they could stay in Ireland and most probably die of starvation. Nonnie and Mary sailed from Cobh to Liverpool and then on to New York, where they set up home in Brooklyn alongside other Irish immigrants and black families, some of whom were former slaves and their children.

Nonnie was fortunate and found work quite quickly as a servant girl for a wealthy family in Brooklyn. Her employers were kind and treated her like one of their own. In return she worked hard for them for nearly forty years, although she always yearned for Templemore and saved carefully for the day when she might be able to return. Mary, on the other hand, met a local man, married him and settled in upstate New York. As time passed, it became clear that their father, increasingly older and weaker back in Templemore, could no longer manage on his own. Finally the sisters said a tearful goodbye on the docks of New York and Nonnie set sail for Ireland, just in time to experience the devastation that the Black and Tans were visiting on her home. When she arrived back in Templemore she brought with her many happy memories of her time in Brooklyn. She also brought back a tidy sum of money, since she had learned thrift early in life. There were times when she regretted her decision to come back but she never changed her mind.

Nonnie watched the arrangements in Oliver's household carefully and did not approve of Oliver's treatment of his family. Nora's neighbours were also aware of the situation but most did not even have enough food or clothes for themselves. Nonnie had enough to share and, because she had worked so very hard all her life and never married, she thought that she was lucky to be able to take

Nora and her children under her wing as if they were her own. When her father died, she drew even closer to Nora's little brood. Her generosity and kind nature saved them from many a hungry night because she never failed to share all the meat, potatoes and vegetables that she could spare. She knew that if she gave them money it would all go on luxuries for Oliver or, worse, on drink.

Nora was deeply grateful to Nonnie for all her support. She often accepted her gifts of food but she did not like to ask every day. On those days when there was no food at all, the children loved to play a game invented by Nora. She would gather them around her and together they would imagine all the wonderful things they would eat if they had all the choice in the world. In their mind's eye, if not in reality, there was always enough for them all.

'Come on, children,' Nora would say. 'I will tell you a bedtime story. Imagine a big plate heaped with mashed potatoes with lashings of butter and a great pile of rashers of bacon. . . .'

'Yes,' little Ollie would say, his eyes gleaming. 'And afterwards a big trifle, with cream and fruit.'

'I'm sure,' Nora would assure the children, 'that one day very soon Daddy will bring us all home a lot of money and then . . . then we will have a feast and eat until our bellies hurt.'

Nora did not yet know that Oliver had another trick up his sleeve. He had been communicating with his great-aunt, Miss Fitzgerald, who lived in Durban, South Africa, and had taken quite a fancy to the idea of a trip to the faraway land.

Miss Gertrude Winifred Fitzgerald was a remarkable lady, respected and revered in Templemore for her incredible courage and successful business life. She had emigrated alone to South Africa in the late 1850s, after being orphaned and left with a large inheritance at the tender age of only twenty. Even at such a young age and with no experience of travel, Miss Fitzgerald (as she was always called) demonstrated remarkable foresight combined with nerves of steel. In those days Irish women simply did not travel on their own, even to the next county, and those who did were seen as fair game by any passing scoundrel who might want to take advantage of them. Who knows how young Gertrude managed to survive that journey without suffering any serious difficulties or without being divested of the considerable sum of money she was carrying? But she was a young woman who always did things on her own terms and she had resolved to seize life by the scruff of the neck and take her chances just like a man.

She never married. Instead she devoted her life to creating a very prestigious hotel in a magnificent building that dominated Durban. She designed and built it herself during the South African gold rush of the late nineteenth century and no expense was spared. Every last detail was meticulously planned, down to the marble floors throughout and the lavish furnishings. As she neared the end of her life she was already looking to the future of her precious business and her ambition was to hand over the reins of her creation to someone in her own family.

Oliver was the eldest of his father's children and she had heard good things about him over the years, so she wrote and asked him if he would like to come out and be trained up as hotel manager. Miss Fitzgerald believed she was choosing wisely. She knew that Oliver had fought in the war and worked in Manchester before moving home to Templemore with his Tipperary wife. She imagined that his war record and his career in Manchester proved that he was brave, ambitious and worldly wise. The fact that he had met and married an Irishwoman in a foreign land seemed to demonstrate that he was a loyal relative and had a strong sense of family values. She was also aware that times were hard in Ireland and she badly wanted to offer a young, deserving member of her family the chance to achieve the success she had known in her own life.

This was the opportunity that Oliver had been dreaming of. He would move away from Ireland's grey skies and his constant financial woes and he would go to the promised land of South Africa to make his fortune there. There was no doubt in his mind that this new, exotic environment would be just what he needed to achieve the success he had always felt he deserved. He even promised Nora that he would finally be able to stop drinking and wasting his money.

'This will be a new chapter in our life,' he told Nora. 'You'll see, love. This is going to be the making of us. I promise you! I'll go out first and make some money and very soon you and the children will be packing your bags and following on.'

'I hope so,' Nora said warily. She didn't want to get her hopes up. Oliver had promised her so much in the past and had delivered none of it.

'This time things will be different,' Oliver said confidently. 'It's a new country where there are opportunities for everyone and this is an established business with money coming in every day. I'll work hard and in a little while we will all be living there, under the sun. You'll see.'

For the first time since shortly after her wedding day Nora began to truly hope that things would improve for herself and the children. Perhaps Oliver was about to become the husband she had always hoped he would be? Perhaps the children would finally have the father they deserved? She resolved to do whatever she could to support him in this new venture. After all, what had she to lose? She was expecting her fifth child and dreaded the thought of another mouth to feed.

In the weeks before his departure Oliver stood every night at the fireplace in their small house to practise his songs, 'My little grey home in the west' and 'The old rugged cross'. He felt sure that his talents would often be called upon in the fine hotel in South Africa. Nora, with her musical gift, checked him when he went off-key and helped him to perfect each tune. Despite Oliver's greater confidence she was the one who really knew how to sing and they both knew it; this was the only reason that he submitted to her instruction.

The children hated it when Oliver sang because they knew it meant that they would be saying goodbye to their daddy soon. Despite his erratic, often drunken behaviour, his callousness and his occasional outbursts of violence, he still was the only father they had and they loved him very dearly. Two-year-old Kitty was still the baby of the family, but even she found the arrangements for her daddy's departure unsettling. How would Mammy manage without Daddy? Eight-year-old Ollie knew exactly what was happening and lay in his bed at night staring at the ceiling and wondering. He knew that his daddy was not a good provider and he had already learned not to trust him, but Oliver was all they had. How would his mother manage to feed them without even the irregular income that he managed to bring home from the cobbler's? He thought about the other children on the street and in the neighbourhood who had had to say 'goodbye' to their fathers, as many had left for foreign shores in search of work. How sorry he had felt for them when they were sad and lonely. His daddy was often cross and he was often drunk, but at least he was there for him, in Templemore. Now *his* father would be leaving, too. But perhaps he would send money back to them and they wouldn't have to have any more imaginary feasts? Perhaps when his daddy became a big success in the sun there would be food on the table every day?

Oliver was remarkably unmoved by grief as he waved goodbye to his family and followed in his great-aunt's footsteps, taking the road from Templemore down to the harbour at Cobh. All he could think of was the glorious future that he was sure lay ahead of him, the money he was certain to make – and the many beautiful women who would line up to throw themselves into his open arms. Not a thought went back down the road to his own children who were already pining for him and wondering when they would see him again. Kicking the dust of the little town and his responsibilities off his feet, he was like a man released from a prison sentence. The sensation was the same as the day he had set off to the Great War: excitement mixed with uncertainty.

*

His intentions may have been good but, as was the usual way with Oliver, the grand plan was scuppered by his own arrogance, selfishness and complete inability to shoulder his responsibilities.

In the beginning Miss Fitzgerald was very happy with Oliver's progress and his business sense. He was bright and quick to learn and managed to charm her in the same way that he had charmed so many others in the past. They seemed to get on well and she had no doubt that she had chosen correctly in selecting him to be her heir. He certainly looked the part of hotel manager: his tall, striking figure seemed naturally to command respect. And, although he had been a heavy drinker for the last couple of years, his appearance was still youthful, with his black, wavy hair combed back from his face. Miss Fitzgerald's refined clientele certainly would not have guessed in a million years that her elegant hotel manager's wife was back in Ireland wondering where the next meal was coming from and spending her evenings repairing her children's ragged clothes and lining the soles of their shoes with cardboard in a futile attempt to keep the water out.

In fact everything went so very well in the beginning that soon Oliver began to take responsibility for the daily running of the hotel and Miss Fitzgerald began to take some time off and rest a little, as befitted a lady of her age. Yes, she thought, life was definitely better with Oliver around. She trusted him and relaxed into giving him responsibility. In return, he was good to her and looked after everything at the hotel as if it was his own. Of course, he was already dreaming of the future, when he *would* own the hotel and would actually be living the role of wealthy hotelier. He worked long, hard hours each day without complaining and in the evening he entertained the hotel guests with his wonderful singing voice and the songs that Nora had taught him so carefully. The exquisite brandy and champagne only served to make the entertaining hotel manager even more hospitable and charming.

*

Back in Templemore Ollie often thought about his father. 'He will be back soon,' he reassured himself. 'He won't be away too long. He will bring us all lovely presents that none of the other children will have and we will be so proud of him.' He tried hard not to cry and feel sad but his grief was always there. He began to find it difficult to remember his father's face, his smell, or the way he walked and held himself. Why had Daddy gone away? Why couldn't he have found a job at home in Templemore like most of the other daddies? Above all, why was he not sending money home to Mammy, as he had promised? When he had left, Mammy had told the children that they would no longer need to worry about a thing because Daddy had a fine new job and would be sending them lots of money. And then, when the time came, he would call for them all to join him in a sunny country far away where they would be happy and rich.

But the money did not come. The children still wore old, threadbare clothes with the hems endlessly turned down and Nora often had to eke out the potatoes and cabbage to make sure that everybody had something to eat. She frequently had to go to Nonnie's house, smiling apologetically in her embarrassment and shame, and ask if there were any vegetables to spare, as there was nothing for the children's meal. She was getting thin. Baby Seamus had been born and the effort of feeding him, while taking as little food as possible for herself, had left Nora anaemic and weak. Her teeth were loose and her lovely hair was already turning grey.

'When is that husband of yours going to send for you and the children?' Nonnie would ask. 'He should be taking care of you and if he doesn't send money, he should make sure that you are with him.'

'Soon, God willing,' was Nora's standard reply. 'I'm sure that he will write for us very soon.'

*

In Durban Oliver was having the time of his life. After dinner he enjoyed a good cigar and brandy with the gentlemen guests who were always ready to accept him into their number because he was so elegant and well-spoken that he seemed the epitome of class. 'Smoke to the clouds,' his aunt would say, reminding Oliver that his role was not just to entertain the gentlemen guests but also to ensure that her beautiful hotel was always kept perfectly. 'Keep the windows well open and let out that fog of smoke.'

On his aunt's instructions Oliver would open up the full-length French windows to let the cigar smoke out into the warm South African air. Then, when the guests had all retired for the night, he would go out to the balcony overlooking the city, although there was not much to see at night except the lights from the ships in dock. There he would lean on the railings and gaze out into the darkness. He rarely thought of Nora and the little ones at home or wondered what they were doing while he enjoyed the temperate night air of Durban. Perhaps he was in denial and pushed the knowledge that he had walked away from a family that needed him back into his subconscious.

The months passed and became years. When he had arrived, Oliver's aunt had reminded him that he was there to work as she saw fit and that he should do all he could to keep the hotel running smoothly in the knowledge that one day it would be his, making him a very wealthy man. She had also made it very clear that if he did not do as she required he would be shipped back to Ireland with nothing. So far Oliver had seemed to be fulfilling his side of the bargain more than adequately. He was fairly paid and his great-aunt assumed that he was sending money back to Templemore on a regular basis.

But eventually Miss Fitzgerald began to wonder how Oliver's family was coping in Ireland without a father in the home. He had now been away from them for two years and she thought it very odd that he never mentioned them at all. At first she had thought that perhaps he did not speak of them because he missed them, but once he was settled and clearly enjoying his life in South Africa she started to have her doubts and wondered if he had actually just forgotten them. Finally she began to quiz him whenever she could to find out exactly what was happening back in Ireland.

'Don't they find it hard, living in a small town?' she asked. She herself could remember, with a shudder, the twitching curtains and people's small-town habit of always wanting to know everything about everyone. She knew that she would never have been able to stay in such an environment.

When Oliver failed to provide the information she requested, Miss Fitzgerald managed to convince herself that at least his family did not have to cope with the poverty that she knew was blighting many families in Ireland: he was, of course, sending money back for them every month. However it *was* strange that he hardly seemed interested when the subject of his family was raised. She remained blissfully ignorant of the fact that the contrast between Oliver's life and that of his family could not have been greater. Every morning Oliver put on a clean white suit and shirt, all prepared for him by his personal maid, a pretty black girl who had caught his eye, and proceeded to live the high life for yet another day. The once-beautiful girl from Tipperary was a distant memory. As for her children, when he had lived at home he had managed to be fond of them on Sundays, when they were clean and brushed and his hangover had subsided. Now they were all but forgotten.

*

The tongues of Templemore, meanwhile, were beginning to wag. Most of the fathers who worked away from

Ireland managed to send home a little money once in a while and there was usually a letter every week, as well as presents at Christmas. Oliver sent nothing. Now people began to say that he was never coming home, that he had abandoned his family for good. The gossip became vicious. While Nora struggled to put food on the table and to care for her family, people told each other that perhaps Nora and Oliver had not really ever been married at all. After all, if they really had been lawfully wed, surely Oliver's family would feel duty-bound to do all they could to support her. But resources were also scarce in the large McManus household and Oliver's parents preferred to turn a blind eye. Their wonderful son could do no wrong and they were sure that Nora's troubles had been brought on by her own failure as a wife.

The children were often teased by their classmates, who accused them of being fatherless. This was a code for 'illegitimate', which was a shameful state; many illegitimate children were sent to live in institutions, far away from their natural parents. There they were instructed that they were the fruit of sin and that their souls were stained as a result. These accusations of illegitimacy were so upsetting that Kitty and her siblings took to inviting their little friends in to see Daddy's picture hanging over the fireplace, just to prove that Oliver really existed. Nora saw her children's shame and would always play her part, telling their friends that the children's father was very brave to travel so far to provide for them. It broke her heart to lie about her husband and to pretend that he cared when she herself had begun to believe that he had deserted her. She prayed that soon Miss Fitzgerald would realise that Oliver's earnings never reached his children's stomachs and that she would force him to provide for the little ones.

7

Flight of the McManus family

The crash of 1929 hit the little town of Templemore badly and the McManus family business, already faltering for several years, finally collapsed. Oliver's parents felt they had no choice but to start over again. It was not an easy decision but they knew that they might have better opportunities in Canada where two of the daughters, Kate and Nora, had already settled. Martin McManus travelled twice to Canada and stayed a month each time in order to make sure that this was the correct choice. Finally the entire family left Ireland for good in 1930, when Kitty was less than four years old. It must have been an expensive journey, a journey towards which Martin had probably been saving privately for several years until the final sale of his shoemaking business made it possible. Ships' passenger lists and border records show their progress to their new home until the whole family, mother, father, siblings and spouses, was installed in Ottawa, next door to Kate. Twelve McManuses left Templemore that year. They would remain in the same place for generations until eventually there were McManuses up and down the street.

Nora took the news of their emigration badly, in spite of the fact that Oliver's kin had never shown her much care or support. She feared that when Oliver heard his family had emigrated he would be less inclined to return to Templemore. And she still had the dream of that happy life somewhere else. She wished with all her heart that she could just take her children and follow the whole clan, perhaps find a job and a little happiness for them all. She knew that Canada was open to immigrants and it was easier to get citizenship there than in the United States. Many others in Templemore were making the same journey to escape poverty at home.

*

Oliver had always had an eye for women and this would be his downfall in Durban. He had slept around for two years but had always managed to keep his affairs quiet. Finally there came a day when Miss Fitzgerald discovered him in bed with her private nurse. She began to make discrete enquiries with the rest of her staff and was shocked when the extent of his debauchery was revealed. Immediately she called him into her office.

'I'm having your bags packed for you,' Miss Fitzgerald said, 'and I've booked a ticket for you on the next ship leaving Port Natal. Get yourself back to your wife and family. They've not seen you for two years and must have been eagerly awaiting your return for months. And what would your lovely wife, Nora, think of your involvement with these other women? I could write to her, you know. I'm sure she would be unhappy to know of the things I've seen in my hotel. How dare you do such a thing and think you could get away with it? I've no need for you anymore as you are nothing like the man I thought you were. I trusted you, your family trusted you, and you let us all down by getting up to mischief with my staff. Did you honestly think that I wouldn't hear about your affairs? You're a wicked, immoral man and you should be ashamed of yourself!

'And think of your children. They love you and need their father. I brought you here on the understanding that you would send money home to support them and bring them over to live with you.'

Oliver hung his head during this tirade, but remained silent.

'Didn't you miss your family?' Miss Fitzgerald continued. 'Did you ever send them money and let them know that you loved them? I suppose you never sent a penny. I feel sorry for them, God help them.

You have spent two years here learning the day-to-day workings of my hotel and I thought you were good at what you were doing. Well, I feel like a very foolish old woman today. Little did I know what was happening behind my back! I shudder to think how close I came to giving you everything – you, who are not even worthy of working as a boot boy in my business. And to think that I wanted to make you my heir! Well, I hope you're happy now. You could have been a very wealthy man indeed. But, instead, you are going home with nothing more than you brought.'

Miss Fitzgerald knew she could not compromise. A man like Oliver would quickly destroy her standing in the community – not to mention the trail of bastard children he might leave behind amongst her chambermaids. She had relied on him to maintain her flourishing business when she was gone, happy to think of him leaving the hotel to his own children when the time came. She had come to love him like a son, the scoundrel that he was.

She knew that a part of her would always love him, in spite of what he had done. That was the danger – and that was why she had to pack him off to Ireland as quickly as possible.

And so Oliver returned to the country he had believed he would never see again, leaving without a second thought for his great-aunt's feelings. Not long after his departure Miss Fitzgerald began to feel unwell. She put it down to the shock of discovering Oliver's misdemeanours and tried to ignore the implications for her health, given her advanced years. But she found that she had no energy to do anything. She stopped going to town in her automobile each day and, just a few hours after rising, she would ask her private nurse to turn down the bed for her and close the curtains so that she could sleep for the rest of the day. This was very unlike the lady the staff knew and loved, and they found her afternoon naps increasingly worrying. The private nurse advised Miss Fitzgerald to call her doctor and, after several days of nagging on the nurse's part, Miss Fitzgerald finally called her doctor one morning after breakfast. He came straight away, gave her some injections, and told her to rest for the next few days because she had a fever. He said that the best place for her was in her warm, comfortable bed. He expected her to make a full recovery and assured her that she had nothing to be anxious about. She stayed in bed for two nights, but on the third she woke with a dreadful pain in her chest – and she had slipped away before anyone could do anything for her.

During her lifetime Miss Fitzgerald's lovely hotel had taken shape exactly as she had wished. Now her lawyer followed her instructions for her own funeral to the letter. Her beloved staff walked on each side of the horse-drawn hearse, covered with her favourite flowers, as she was carried to her final resting place in a grave looking out over Port Natal. Her many mourners trailed behind weeping and regretting the life that had ended so abruptly. Afterwards everyone spoke tearfully of the way in which she had planned to spend her retirement years travelling around her adopted land in her chauffeured car. She had dreamed of seeing all the sights and doing all the things that she had not been able to do during her many years of hard work. Now none of those dreams would be fulfilled. Most people felt that the nature of Oliver's departure had at least hastened her demise.

*

Night after night on the journey home Oliver entertained the passengers at the captain's table, talking to the finest ladies and gentlemen on the ship. His wonderful singing voice earned him money but he lost it all again, gambling it away at the roulette table and spending the rest on expensive champagne to impress whichever lady had caught his eye on that particular evening. He convinced himself he didn't care.

Eventually, there he was, walking up the street in Templemore as if he had never been away. His children were out playing with the neighbours' sons and daughters, but Ollie was the first to see him coming. He looked and looked again. Yes! It was Daddy!

'Mammy!' he shouted, running into the house. 'Daddy is coming down the street.'

Nora went pale with a combination of shock and excitement. She ran to the mirror to fix her hair and pinch her cheeks to give them a bit of colour. She waited inside the front door and as soon as Oliver entered she hugged and kissed him.

'Welcome home, Oliver,' she said, 'How are you? We've been waiting for you for a long time. You haven't even met the baby yet . . . he's not a baby now, of course, he can walk and everything . . .'

'I'm glad to be home,' he replied with a sigh. 'Oh God, South Africa is so hot it's unbearable and the journey really takes it out of you. It will take me a few weeks to get back on my feet after all this travelling.'

'Sit down there, Oliver,' Nora said, pulling him towards a chair, 'and I will make a nice cup of tea for you. I'll wake the baby from his nap so that you can see him. I want to hear everything. Did you come to bring us back to South Africa with you? When are we going to leave?'

'Ah, not at all, Nora. Don't bother with the tea. I'll just pop down to see the lads at Flynn's house, as they're waiting for me to call in for a few jars. I met some of them on the street as I got off the train. I won't be long. Don't wake the baby on my behalf; let him have his sleep. It's a boy, isn't it? Stay up and wait for me and then we'll talk about everything . . .'

And Oliver was gone. He did not come home again until the sun was beginning to rise the following morning.

Nobody knew exactly what had happened in Africa and Oliver was not going to tell them. The excuse he always gave for his return was that he did not like the heat and the lifestyle. 'What is more,' he would say. 'I missed my wife and family. I wanted to come back to my lovely Nora and my beautiful children.'

Having no reason not to believe him, Nora swallowed this lie but her hopes and dreams for their inheritance were shattered. She knew things were not going to become any easier. The children, who did not understand how difficult life was going to be, were simply happy to see their daddy back and to be able to show their classmates that they did have a father, after all. Too young to understand what they had lost, they continued to wear their threadbare clothes and learned again how to be quiet on those nights when daddy came home drunk, for fear of aggravating him.

Soon, another baby was on the way. Then there were six: Ollie, Betty, Johnny, Kitty, Seamus and Richard. Oliver was sad to hear that twelve members of his family had set sail for Canada. It made him think again about distant shores, but for the moment he knew he had no choice but to stay in Templemore. He felt trapped and regretted blowing everything in South Africa. He often dreamed of being back there but kept up his lie that he had hated the place. It was difficult settling back into the small town and he felt like a stranger in his own home. He looked at his wife, and she was old and worn out before her time. He saw his children pale and thin, but it wasn't enough to make him stop drinking. Drink was his only escape.

Two more years passed and Oliver found himself growing restless again. He started to tell anyone who would listen that it was time for him to move on because he was meant for better things. But the truth was that he had realised it was no longer as easy for him to charm the Templemore ladies into bed. He had acquired the reputation of a man who should be avoided at all cost and he had been involved in several fights with local men who blamed him, probably accurately, for being cuckolded by their wives.

Oliver determined that, since Africa had not worked out as he had hoped, he would go to America and make his fortune there instead. Now that the rest of the McManuses had gone to Canada, he did not see any particular reason to stay. With the money he could put together in the form of loans and gifts from friends and relatives who had grown tired of being asked for help and who liked the idea of Oliver leaving town and finally sorting out his life, he bought himself a ticket. He showed it to Nora and told her that he would send for her and the children very soon: 'We'll all be Yanks. I'll buy you a beautiful house and work hard and we'll be rich and happy. Then I will be the husband you deserve, I promise. We will all be happier than you can even begin to imagine.'

Nora smiled wanly. She wanted to believe what Oliver was saying. She wanted that more than anything. But she knew it was going to be hard without him again; she had never grown used to him being away while he was in Africa and she had hated the gossip and rumours that had spread about the nature of their relationship. As bad a husband as Oliver was, Nora loathed the thought of having no one to share the hardships of every day. But she knew that this was how it would be, at least until Oliver called for them to join him in America. So she kept her sorrow from her children and tried to smile her way through every challenge and upset. The loneliness of those dark nights when she lay awake with no partner to comfort and reassure her was a secret she would share with no one.

*

Oliver took a ship to America and spent a few months there 'sorting things out', as he put it. When he came back, the people of Templemore were surprised that the wayward father had at last kept to his promise. Nora herself was so relieved that she dared to believe that their luck might finally change – perhaps her husband had grown up and now wanted to do right by his family? Was it possible that she might start to live every day without worrying where the next mouthful was coming from? That they might have an ordinary, peaceful family life? When he arranged for them all to be vaccinated and to get passports, the wave of excitement and optimism in the house reached fever pitch.

During Oliver's visit their home was full of neighbours each night, all wanting to hear Oliver recount tales of his adventures. The stories he told. Everyone who listened was utterly enthralled by his account of crossing the Atlantic and how he had got a job singing with the orchestra and made a fortune in tips from the fine ladies who were dressed so elegantly for dinner. He had even been invited to sit at the captain's table, he said, although he and the other musicians were sleeping in the belly of the boat, the lowliest quarters of all.

'I have no trouble travelling,' Oliver said grandly, 'but there are those who get sick and some who die – oh yes, quite a few never even step onto the wharf at New York. But not this bucko. I'd travel to the ends of the earth for me and mine.'

While Oliver basked in the limelight, Nora would brew tea and prepare the sandwiches that her uninvited guests seemed to expect without giving a thought to how she would find the money for the ingredients.

And then there came a night, long after the neighbours had fallen merrily out the door, when Oliver reached for Nora in bed and she pushed his hand away.

'We can't do anything like that,' she said. 'Not any more. The doctor told me I'm not to have any more children. It's already damaged my health too much and he says another baby could be the death of me.' Abstinence was the only way for the women of Templemore in those days, since contraception was unheard of and, in any case, unavailable.

Oliver said nothing. He simply rolled over in bed and fell asleep, breathing heavily. A week later he left.

*

On the day of Oliver's departure it seemed that all the town had come out to bid him farewell and he put on a great show of kissing his wife and children before the onlookers, promising that he looked forward to returning in one year to take them with him to a new life in a new world. Kitty and her brothers and sisters were so excited and proud. Every child in town was finally looking at the McManuses with envy. *Their* daddy was heading back to America – the land of opportunity – and soon he was going to come back and take his family with him and they would all embark upon a grand new life. As he walked away he looked, to their eyes, as if he were a retreating hero.

Long after he had left they continued to speak of him in worshipful tones. Daddy had told them so much about America that the children felt as if they could already picture it: how they would feel when they started school, what their house would be like, what they would eat. Although they were sad at the thought of leaving all their friends and neighbours, they started to prepare for the new adventure that lay ahead. In a year's time Daddy would come back and collect them and they would step into a wonderland in which Daddy and Mammy were happy and rich and there was always enough to eat.

Every week they expected to get a letter from Oliver telling them that he was on his way. Months passed. The children in the street started to ask, 'Is your daddy *ever* going to come home to get you and bring you to America? We think you're all lying to us, that he's not coming back for you at all.' Despite the children's insistence that, yes, Daddy would be coming back soon, no word came from Daddy – no letter or telegram to say he was on the way.

Nora became increasingly uneasy. She worried that their passports and papers might expire or their vaccinations might wear off. She could not understand what the delay could be. Gradually she began to worry that this time he had abandoned them for good and would never come home. She did not want to believe it and at first she resisted the thought. But it came back, unbidden, and soon it filled her mind.

After a year Nora was sure that this was it. He was gone and he was never going to come back for them – never. But the children continued to hope that Daddy would return, although they stopped speaking of this hope even amongst themselves. Their mother often wondered if Oliver had started drinking heavily over there. Perhaps he was so deeply in debt again that he couldn't afford to send money and was ashamed to contact them? She even wondered if he might be dead. She knew what he was like when he was drinking: death in a drunken brawl or an accident when he was drunk was all too likely.

*

Soon the younger children could no longer remember their father's face. Although she had given up all hope of ever seeing her husband again, Nora continued to go to the post office, day after day, week after week. After a while the postman pre-empted her question: 'Nothing today, I'm afraid, Mrs McManus. We'll deliver it when it comes, don't you worry.' Every time she returned from the post office the children would notice that her face was paler, her step more hopeless. Time began to play cruel tricks with her young woman's body and her face grew more lined and care-worn. Time and alcohol, for in her bitterness and grief Nora herself had begun to drink.

Oliver's family never heard from him again. Eventually Nora convinced herself that she knew the reason why. In later years, when her daughters were women, she would tell them about their father and his insatiable sexual desires. 'He could not live without it,' she would say, 'and I could not give it to him.' She had been a bad wife. As a good Catholic woman she should have known better; she should have obeyed her husband as she had promised on her wedding day and as the local priest insisted every woman should, because it was God's will for women that they should submit themselves to their husbands. Even if another pregnancy had risked her life, she should have given in to Oliver's advances. What had she been thinking?

The family was now destitute. If Nora had been a widow, she would have been entitled to some help from the state. As an abandoned wife she was entitled to nothing at all because her husband was still morally and legally responsible for supporting his wife and family. Not only that, but Nora also attracted the suspicion that her abandonment was somehow her fault, that perhaps she was an immoral woman. Surely a man would not abandon the mother of his children without a reason?

Over and over she tried to contact the McManuses in Canada, using the last address she had had for them. Because she knew that her children were Martin's grandchildren she refused to give up, sending letter after letter in the hope that they might finally take pity on her and help her to find Oliver. Or at least tell her if he was dead or alive. But there was never a word in reply; it was as if the McManuses had ceased to exist.

Nora kept her thoughts to herself but, as her children grew, they began to understand their mother's depression and rejection. They felt rejected too. Great-aunt Nonnie was the only person in the world to whom she could turn. However, although Nonnie could provide a listening ear and some material help, she could not help Nora find any hope for the future.

8

Young lives and an old feud

School offered little Kitty some reprieve from the misery that hung over her home. The local girls' school stood opposite Kitty's house; a huge building, painted white, with scores of windows facing out to the street and a vast, impressive entrance door in the centre. The yard around the school was immense, but it did not invite play or happy times. Most of the girls who attended school with Kitty in the hungry decade of the 1930s would grow up to have very few good memories of their education.

In those years, and for many years to come, most of the teachers in Ireland were nuns and Christian Brothers, and they were hard masters who beat and slapped the children more than even the toughest parent. Many of them did even worse than that. It seems that they believed they had the God-given right to torment children, whom they saw as their social inferiors.

The nuns who taught in Kitty's school were no different: they lived by the rod and considered it the best method of imparting information and keeping their young charges quiet. Whatever affection and respect they had in their withered hearts was reserved for the daughters of big farmers and the wealthier of the small businessmen who owned the shops and small factories in the town. The children were taught favouritism in action. The nuns might curry favour with the rich pupils and their parents, but the poorer students were repeatedly told that they were no good, worthless, foolish and that the Virgin Mary herself would weep when she saw what useless lumps they were. To the nuns these children were simply little souls who were to be marched into church, at the appropriate times, for the provision of the sacraments. When no one was administering to their souls, they were fair game for any slapping, hair-pulling and ear-tugging that the nuns chose to deliver.

In spite of this Kitty liked school, although she was never one of the favourites. Many of the other children internalised the fierce lessons they were taught and behaved accordingly, but Kitty always knew that she was strong and that she would survive. She was not unlike her great grand-aunt Miss Fitzgerald. At a very young age Kitty had already resolved to do everything in her power to become a woman capable of standing alone. She was determined that, when the time came, she would make a good life for herself and her family and fulfil her hopes and dreams.

Kitty was always one of the first to arrive at school in the morning, together with her older sister Betty. Their little house was so near that they just had to run out the front door and they were practically there. The two girls were in adjacent classrooms that were divided by a glass partition and they often sneaked glances at each other through the glass. Of course, this was strictly prohibited by the nuns and they were punished whenever they were caught, but the temptation to see what was going on next door was always there.

Kitty was a lively child and very popular with the other children, who envied her ability to question the teachers. The teachers themselves were less appreciative, since Kitty would frequently ask questions that they were unable to answer. Then she would look at them guilelessly, secretly smiling because she had put them on the spot. Since the rest of the class clearly enjoyed the spectacle, and Kitty herself was obviously unafraid of the nuns' threats and punishments, the nuns disliked Kitty even more.

One day Kitty was worrying about the good Lord Jesus. In the middle of religion class, she put up her hand to ask a question.

'What is it now, child?' asked Sister Agnes impatiently, pointing at Kitty. 'Why do you always disrupt my class, especially when we are all silent and listening to the word of God?'

Kitty stood up.

'I have a question for you, sister. Why does God punish us when we die? He is supposed to be all-forgiving. He tells us to forgive everyone, all our neighbours and friends. But if *we* do anything wrong or sin, when we get to the gates of Heaven he will judge us and not forgive us. He will punish us and send us to Hell for our sins.'

Kitty looked at her teacher anxiously. She very much wanted the answer to this question – and to many more – as she was a very inquisitive child. Sister Agnes stood as straight as a rod and thought for a moment or two, her head high and her eyes turned skyward; she fixed her headdress. Then she turned slowly towards the window, looking out across the schoolyard and beyond. Once again she found herself at a loss to answer little Kitty's infernal questions. All the children were cringing in their seats, waiting for an outburst. There was not a sound in the classroom - you could hear a pin drop.

'Kitty McManus,' Sister Agnes eventually roared. 'What devil put that idea in your head? Is it the devil himself working through you today? Why do you always interrupt my class with your incessant questions?'

'No, sister,' Kitty replied. 'I'm not being bold. It's just that I have been thinking about God and the way he works and I don't understand why he should punish anyone when he himself is all-forgiving.'

Sister Agnes could not answer Kitty.

'Would you just sit down in your desk,' she shouted, 'Listen to the word of God and do not query it again.'

These exchanges always ended in much the same way. The teacher who had just been shown up would shout, 'Kitty McManus, stop your impudence and go and stand in the corner and think about your behaviour. You should be ashamed of yourself! Keep your mouth shut! Don't you look at me like that, young lady. Behave yourself or you will be getting a good hiding from me.'

Kitty's sister Betty was a timid child who never argued back and unfortunately the nuns often classed her as a troublemaker too, because of her clever, outspoken sister's behaviour. She always quietly took the blame. Then later, at home, she would beg, 'Would you ever stop being so bold, Kitty, it brings all the attention on me and I hate it.'

This infuriated Kitty, who would give out to her for her retiring ways: 'Why do you take that from those stupid nuns? Why do you let them walk all over you? You should give them a taste of their own medicine!' Kitty was always impatient with those whom she saw as weak.

'I'm scared of the nuns!' Betty would say. 'They are always so cross.'

'*Feck* the nuns,' Kitty would answer boldly, not caring who heard her. 'I'm sure God doesn't like the nuns because of the way they treat us girls. Do you think God told the nuns that they should beat us? I don't think that God would do something like that! I think the nuns have God all wrong. I think they're talking through their holy arses, so I do!'

In Betty's class the children sat two to a desk and, one day, her companion carved her initials into the wood of the surface. Betty was blamed although she had not done it. Terrified of the furious nun, she said nothing to defend herself. That evening she went home and showed Nora her sore hands, where she had been beaten.

Nora was furious. She was fiercely protective of her children and would not let anyone, least of all the nuns, belittle or blame any of them for crimes they had not committed. She put on her coat and marched over to the school, demanding to see Sister Margaret, the nun in question. She made her way down every corridor until she found her and, when she did, she gave Sister Margaret more than the nun had bargained for. These hard women, used to working with children who could not defend themselves, were less tough when it came to a mother filled with righteous indignation and the fierce protective instinct that is part and parcel of motherhood. Sister Margaret never blamed Betty for anything again. In fact, she barely even acknowledged her presence after that, which suited the shy child very well.

Despite her rebellious streak and her habit of getting into trouble, Kitty was very bright. She infuriated the nuns further by always having her homework completed, her spellings done and her tables memorised. She loved to read and devoured anything that came her way, from discarded newspapers to whatever book she happened upon. The nuns hated the fact that Kitty was so good at her schoolwork; because she was a difficult pupil from a troubled family, it seemed only right that she should be a weak student as well. They checked her homework meticulously and rebuked her strongly for the slightest flaw, although hers was generally the best work in the class. What they did not realise was that the harder they were on her the more resolved Kitty became to be the best that she could. By the time she reached the final years of school, she had grown more knowledgeable than many of the nuns and was able to correct them when they slipped up with their spelling or their sums. And so, with each passing year, they disliked her even more.

*

Kitty excelled in religious studies and, although she was not fond of the nuns, was deeply religious in an unquestioning, childish way. She fervently recited her prayers every morning and night and truly believed that if she prayed long and hard and did her best to be a good girl for her mother, God would be pleased with her and would help to make her life a little better. Whenever she prayed, Kitty never failed to include her heart's desire.

'Dear God,' she would whisper. 'Bless Mammy and Daddy and make Daddy come home to take care of us.' She would look heavenward and clasp her little hands even harder.

'If you are up there, God, please listen and hear my prayers. I need you to help get my Daddy to come home to us all. Mammy needs him and we do too. Please, please hear my prayers and do something to make him come home. Our Mammy is lonely, we see her sitting alone with no one to talk to. Give me a sign that you know about us and how lonely we are without our Daddy, and Mammy so sad.'

She always felt a bit better after asking God to help the family, even though things did not improve. She felt that she was talking to someone who would listen and, one day, help them. What else could she do, other than pray every day?

Even after he had been gone for several years, Kitty still lay in her bed at night and dreamed of what would happen when her daddy came home. She was sure that he would come into the school and rebuke the nuns for being so mean to his little girl. If Daddy came home, Kitty reasoned, Mammy would be happier and she would not need to drink anymore and there would be money to pay for all the food the family could eat.

'Perhaps,' Kitty told herself, 'one day he will turn up out of the blue and be a father to me and my sister and brothers, and a proper husband for Mammy. He might be lying in a hospital bed somewhere, desperate to find us, but with his memory lost . . .'

Kitty tried hard to remember her father's face, but unless she was looking at his picture on the wall she was finding it increasingly difficult to recall. She knew that he had a moustache. She knew that he had sparkling eyes. But she was not sure that she would recognise him if she saw him on the street.

Despite Kitty's fervent prayers nothing but a resounding silence came from Oliver. The children of Templemore, many of whom had had come with their parents to hear his stories and wave him goodbye when he left, redoubled their teasing of the McManus children, calling them 'bastards' and saying again that they had no father because, if he existed, why was he not taking care of them? Had he found out that they were not really his children at all? Was *that* why he had abandoned them?

Kitty's prayers were not the only prayers to go out from the McManus household every night. Although Nora was increasingly hopeless and exhausted with the effort of providing for her young family, she never failed to gather the children together each evening.

'We will pray for Daddy's safe return from America,' she would say, her head bowed low and pitifully.

But Daddy never came.

*

Things had been bad before, but now they were desperate. Nora sent the children out at night to steal cabbages, potatoes and turnips from the farmers' fields on the outskirts of the town. When there was money, she was often tempted to spend it on drink and the children would find her crying downstairs, propping her head up in her hands and berating herself for having been taken in by a handsome scoundrel.

The neighbours were concerned and decided to call the child welfare officer to do something to help Nora's situation. The child welfare officer was known as the 'cruelty man' and everyone was afraid of him. He wanted to take the children from Nora and put them into care, telling her that this would give her a chance to find work and get her life together. But going into care would have meant going into an industrial school and that was a fate that nobody wanted for their children. Great-aunt Nonnie would have none of it. She made sure that the 'cruelty man' did not take the Kitty and her siblings; it was thanks to her that the young McManuses never had to suffer the long working hours, beatings and sexual abuse that were common in the industrial schools of the time. Bad as home often was, 'care' would have been much worse.

The burden of caring for his anguished mother and bereft siblings fell increasingly on young Ollie's shoulders. When he was only thirteen and still at school, he found a part-time job at a butcher's shop. Although his voice had not yet broken and his face was as smooth as a baby's, he bore this responsibility as well as he could and did his best to act and feel like a grown-up man. Ollie took nothing for himself, giving all his wages to Nora, and was simply pleased whenever he could help his family.

Tinker Brown's family had nurtured and grown their grudge against the descendants of Martin McManus over the years. As Oliver took up his new role as head of the household and the oldest McManus male, he became the new target for the Brown family's wrath against his grandfather. Increasingly they accosted him and beat him black and blue with the warning that there was plenty more where that came from, and that he should not dare to cross them in any way. Although he suffered from severe asthma, he never let this stop him from standing his ground. He often had to fight his way home from school and, in later years, work, because the tinker family lay in wait for him.

In response to the constant threat of being beaten up, Ollie became the toughest youngster in Templemore, protecting his family with fists and kicks and determination. If ever one of the little ones had a scrap with another child, all they had to say was, 'I will get Ollie to go after you!' That usually ended the problem, because Ollie was a force to be reckoned with and everyone in Templemore knew it.

Ollie knew that he would quite likely have to defend himself against the tinkers for the rest of his life, or at least as long as he stayed in Templemore, because they would never forgive the sins of his grandfather. He grew up mentally and physically very quickly; even in his early teens he rightly considered himself the head of the McManus tribe and he would retain that title for years to come.

As he was the eldest, Nora began to treat him as an adult almost as soon as he started work. Although she never wanted to do it, she was often forced to withdraw him from school to work on the bog in Thurles, otherwise there would have been no fuel to warm the house. As soon as he could officially leave school, Ollie went to work full-time for the butcher, which provided him with a regular income for the sixteen long hours of work he did each day. Effectively he worked for nothing, since he gave most of his wages over to his mother. Ollie's only luxury was his fiddle, which he played well, having inherited his mother's musical gift.

With Ollie bringing some money into the household things were a little easier – but only a little.

'I should have married a farmer,' Nora often remarked bitterly to him when they sat alone by the fire at the end of another long day. 'Farmers' families never go hungry.'

'You're not wrong there,' Ollie would say. 'They have all the food they want to eat. And you should see the fine, fat animals they bring in for the butcher to slaughter. They have meat to eat every day! They're so lucky, they don't know they are born.'

'Well,' said Nora philosophically. 'Now that you are working at the butcher's, at least you can bring me home the odd bag of bones so that I can make soup.'

Ollie was protective of his mother and did all he could to help her. What Ollie did not tell his younger sisters and brothers was that, after they had all gone to bed at night, he often had to go and collect Nora from the local pub because she was in no fit state to come back on her own.

She had rarely drunk much, as she did not have enough money to do so, but she would drink instead of eating and, with her slender build and the drink on an empty stomach, the alcohol would go straight to her head. Ollie would put her to bed and then go back onto the street to beat up the boys who had taunted him for having to carry his drunken mother back to the house in full view of all the neighbours. After every drunken episode Nora stayed in the house for a week or so until the gossip had died down, but the tongues of Templemore ensured that these episodes were not quickly forgotten.

'Don't you mind those gossip mongers,' Ollie would tell his mother. 'But Mammy, do try to stop drinking. You know that it's bad for you.'

'I should have been born a farmer's daughter,' Nora would say again. 'Then I would have nothing to worry about, and no need to drink.'

And so it went on. As she sat and talked to Ollie or stared into the fire on her own, Nora's thoughts would turn repeatedly, obsessively almost, to her father and his old plan to marry her off to the wealthy local farmer – how different her life might have been. Farmers did not always have a lot of money but it was true that they generally fared better than the town poor. The farm women were very industrious. They knew how to sew, cook, keep house and bring water from the well.

Although the farm women worked hard, they were generally content with their lot because they could see for themselves the results of their labour. The vegetables they grew fed their children; the hens they raised laid eggs and went into the pot. The bread they cooked, often on an open fire from grain that they had grown and ground themselves, was delicious and nourishing for their sons and daughters. Farmers' children were robust and ruddy and not at all like her own wan, underweight offspring.

And no doubt the farmer was dead by now and she could have been a wealthy landowner in her own right. She also missed her siblings and often thought fondly of her childhood – so different from her own children's lives. Many an example of her father's steadfast support came to her mind in these dark broodings, but his fierce protection of her on one bright spring evening when she had been only twelve stood out above all the others, probably because she had been so very frightened.

Little Nora had been sent to the well for two buckets of water. Although it was evening, the sun was still up in the sky and she was as happy as she could be and content with her life. As she walked, she listened to the birds singing in the trees and the lambs in the fields calling for their mothers. There was a gentle breeze on her face and rays from the warm sun fell on her back. Some dogs were barking in the distance. The well was about a mile away from her house and Nora had skipped happily along, swinging the buckets in her hands.

As she made her way to the well, Nora noticed a farmer she knew sitting under a tree in the distance. His farm was a little way down the road from her family home and his daughter was one of Nora's classmates in school. As she drew near, the man smiled at her slyly.

'Good evening, Miss Langley,' he said. 'Aren't you in a happy mood this evening?'

'I am,' Nora replied. 'It's a lovely day, so it is.'

'So it is,' he repeated.

Nora continued on her way. For some reason the man's smile had made her nervous, and she began to wonder why he had been sitting under the tree. She had never seen him sit there before.

Nora hurried along and filled her buckets with water from the well. She remembered her mother's instructions: 'Take your time, Nora, and bring the buckets home full, not half-empty. I need the water for the washing in the morning.'

As she walked back up the road, Nora stopped now and again to rest and set the buckets down on the road. She saw that the neighbour was still under the tree.

'What will he say to me this time?' she thought. 'I will pass along as quickly as I can. I won't look at him at all.'

As Nora drew close, she could see the man watching her. His eyes seemed fixed on her face.

'Miss Langley,' he said. 'Come here for a moment. I have something to show you.'

Nora hesitated.

'Come,' he said. 'I won't touch you. There's no need for you to be afraid of me. Sure, you know me well. I only want to show you something.'

Feeling that she should do as she was asked, Nora put the buckets down on the side of the road and went over to her neighbour.

'What is it you want to show me?' she asked. 'Only I'm in a hurry. My mother is waiting for the water to do the washing and I have to be quick.'

'Over here in this tree,' he said. 'Look!'

Nora stepped forward to see what it was.

'There you are,' the man said. 'It's a lovely bird's nest with young chicks inside.'

As he moved the branch of the tree, the little chicks' beaks opened wide in anticipation of food from their mother.

'Look, they are waiting for their mother to come and feed them.'

Now Nora forgot that she was nervous. She loved all animals and was very interested to see the chicks. She looked closer at the nest and the little birds. Suddenly the man caught her about the waist and pulled her close to him. He was breathing heavily and his pupils were dilated in excitement. Nora could smell his foul breath on the back of her neck.

'Let me go!'

She struggled to free herself, but his grasp was too strong. He started fumbling at the buttons on his trousers.

'Let me go!'

Nora was so scared that she started to scream as loudly as she could and struggled harder to free herself. Suddenly Nora's father appeared out of nowhere.

'Stop, stop!' he shouted. 'Let my daughter go, if you know what's good for you! What do you think you are doing? I'll beat the living daylights out of you! Don't touch my daughter.'

Suddenly free, Nora ran towards her father, crying.

'Oh, Daddy,' she said. 'I was so afraid. Thank you for saving me. Were you there all the time?'

'No, Nora,' Tom Langley said grimly. 'I just happened to be passing when I heard someone scream and shout. That man will pay. His wife will know about this. Yes, I will make sure that she knows what kind of a man her husband is, stalking and luring young girls and trying to do bad things to them. That man is well respected around here, but he's shown us his true colours now. As soon as I've told his wife, I'll go to the police station and report him!'

'Please don't get into trouble over me, Daddy,' Nora replied, whimpering.

'Sure, you did nothing, girl. It's that awful man who needs reprimanding. It will be good enough for him to be up in court and made a spectacle of. He'll never touch any young girl again if I have anything to do with it, I'll make sure of it.'

Thanks to Tom Langley, the assailant was brought to the police station that evening and charged with assault, disgracing him in the eyes of the whole community and shaming and embarrassing his wife and children. He tried to clear his name, saying that he did not know what had come over him. He apologised to the Langley family, and to Nora, and promised it would never happen again in his lifetime. As far as Nora was aware, it never had.

Whenever she remembered that terrible evening and the way that her father had appeared like her knight in shining armour, she always felt like weeping for the things she had lost. More than anything she longed for Tom to walk in the door and call her his 'little girl'. He had always been there to protect her; he had been trying to protect her when he had warned her not to marry Oliver, too. Why, oh why, had she refused to listen? Nora thought of Oliver and remembered the beatings he had given her; how shocked, ashamed and vulnerable she had felt. She was not used to violence. Her father might have been hard on his family, but he had beaten neither his wife nor his children. Nora knew that her own children had been scared of their father while he had been living with them, but she did not like to dwell on it. The terrible thing is, she thought, I would still give anything to have him back at home. I'd even put up with his drunken ways and his violence if only he provided his family with some money.

*

Nora wasn't the only one to think how good it would be to live as a farmer. Her own daughter often dreamed of being a farmer's daughter. Kitty's classmates, many of whom were farmers' daughters, told her tales of life at home. Most of these stories revolved around food in one way or another and Kitty imagined their home lives as full of plenty.

The girls from the farms said that once a year each farm family would kill a pig, preserve and smoke the meat, and make delicious black puddings, rich with fat and grease and flavour. They could eat meat every day; the McManuses considered themselves very lucky indeed if they ate it once a week, as they lived mostly on boiled potatoes and cabbage, with little to add flavour or nourishment. And then, when the grain was threshed on the farms, all the neighbours would help one another and a great feast would be held, with home-made bread, pork, bacon and potatoes for twenty hungry men, as well as a fine barrel of beer to ease the work. How Kitty wished that she could befriend a farmer's daughter and be taken home as a guest to eat her fill of all the meat she wanted. She imagined licking the delicious bacon fat from her fingers. But wise little Kitty always managed to remind herself, in the end, how glad she was glad that Ollie had a job and was bringing home more food for the family now.

Town and country people alike were religious and, despite Nora's ferocity towards the nuns who mistreated her daughters, the McManuses, like everyone else, attended Mass in Templemore every Sunday, on holidays and every day during Lent. Choosing not to attend Mass was simply not an option for ordinary families. Sunday was the one day when the McManus children did not envy the farmers because the church was a short stroll away from home for them, but a hearty walk for the families who had to come in from the countryside. Wednesdays and Fridays were fast days, when no meat was supposed to be eaten.

The McManuses' diet was so meagre that this made little difference to them, but the farmers' children noticed the change, with no fine, fat meat on their plates.

Each evening almost every family got down on their knees to pray and say a few decades of the rosary, thanking God and the Virgin Mary for all their help, and calling on the saints to intervene with whatever problems they were having at the time. The McManus family had plenty to pray for and they always observed this tradition. It was hard to keep still during the prayers, especially as Nora insisted that the children stay on their knees on the cold, hard floor. The prayers seemed to go on forever. Each child recited a decade of the rosary. Kitty often rolled her eyes to make her siblings laugh when it was their turn and received a half-hearted clip about the ear for giggling. All the angels and saints in Heaven had to be prayed to after the rosary had been completed, adding another ten minutes to the procedure.

Once a year or so a mission came to Templemore as it did to all the market towns in the county and, once again, there was no question of not attending because the local priest would notice who was there and who was not, and there would be hell to pay for staying at home. The mission, it was said, was God's way of checking up on who was really God-fearing, and who was just paying lip-service to their religion. Everyone lived in fear of the priests' disapproval, although the mission was universally detested. It dragged the farming folk away from their work and disrupted everyone's lives, while also making them feel miserable about themselves and their chances for salvation after death.

Although she was blameless, the cloud of suspicion always hung over Nora and fingers would quickly be pointed if *she* did not go to the missions in Templemore.

Her absence on these occasions would be proof enough for the locals that her husband had abandoned her for being a bad wife, or that perhaps that she had never really been married at all. And so she always cleaned up her children, put on their best clothes and went off to attend for seven or nine days that each mission lasted.

When they were all gathered, the townspeople and farmers alike had to kneel meekly and listen to the priests' ranting about Hell and brimstone and the terrible fate that awaited anyone who did not do exactly what they were told. The adult men and women were almost as frightened of the priests as the children were. They had a way of talking about Hell that made it seem just around the corner, and 'sinners' were told that if they did not confess they would not receive absolution, could not take communion and would go to Hell on the spot if they died. Women were kept in their place at the missions, as they were at home. They had to keep their heads covered, as bare-headed women could not enter the church. Younger women tied a scarf under their chins and older women drew their shawls over their heads on entering the church.

Kitty was always more interested in the stall outside the church, which sold rosary beads, medals, relics, prayer books and the Bible. How she yearned to be able to buy some of these pretty 'holy things'. But, having no money, she could only look longingly at all the lovely items on the stall.

'Mammy,' she would ask. 'Will you give me money to buy those lovely, shiny red rosary beads with the gold cross? I would say an extra rosary every night if I had those beads.'

'Sorry, Kitty,' Nora invariably replied. 'We will have to use our fingers to count and continue praying as usual.

We need all the prayers we can manage to bring Daddy home to us, but we can say them without the beads.'

*

Ollie was a good-looking young man and he had started to go out a little at night to spend time with the other young people and to look at the pretty girls who were interested in him, despite the fact that he was from such a poor family. This called for no small courage on his part because the priests prowled the highways and byways with heavy sticks, ready to beat apart any young couple that might be having a cuddle, or even standing too close together and looking at each other just that little bit too longingly. Matchmaking was still carried out, especially in rural parishes, and the priests had a vested interest in discouraging love matches; this was one of the reasons why they went to such efforts to separate courting couples. Many of the priests were the younger sons of wealthy farmers and marriages were arranged to unite farms and keep the land together. Priests were often called upon to match the daughters and sons of farmers with adjacent territories and they were rewarded handsomely for this work.

'I'm sick of Templemore and the priests!' Ollie would remark to his mother, after yet another night when he or one of his friends had been chased down the road by a priest wielding a walking-stick and shouting dire threats. 'What business is it of theirs if I go for a walk with a girl? And what business is it of theirs if I should go courting with a farmer's daughter? Amn't I as good as anyone else in this town? Every place I go at night, the priests are around. That bloody Father Murphy is everywhere; he has eyes in the back of his head. Wouldn't you think he had something better to do?'

'Hush! Don't say that. Someone might hear you and tell Father Murphy what you've been saying and then we'll be in for it!'

At home Nora scoffed at the priests, but like everyone else she was both afraid and in awe of them. Moreover, when things were very bad at home, she needed to know that she could call on the Church for charity and have a chance of getting some assistance. She had often done so, especially at Christmas when it was easier to get help, although she never told her children about it.

Even with Ollie's help Nora rarely managed to supplement her children's diet with a little meat or anything more nutritious. Consequently, whenever there was a childhood illness doing the rounds, the younger McManus children always caught it first and took longer to recover than their school friends. They often had nits and lice and Nora had to remove them painstakingly with a fine-tooth comb, giving them a good dose of DDT afterwards in the hope that the creatures would not return, although they always did.

Nora felt her family could not sink lower. She knew that she had to swallow her pride and ask for her parents' help. She was their daughter after all, and the children were their grandchildren. Surely they would find it in their hearts to offer her some assistance?

9

Seeking help

Nora's father had never relented. He had continued to maintain that Oliver was not, nor ever would be, good enough for her. The truth was that even if Oliver *had* made her a good husband, Tom Langley was probably stubborn enough to refuse to change his mind.

As a school teacher in a small community, and thus one of the very few educated people in his area, Tom was a man who had grown used to being revered and seen as an authority on most matters by the men and women whom he met every day. His failure to force his wayward daughter to comply with his wishes had devastated and humiliated him, possibly more than any event in his life. He was sure that he had lost face in his community as a result of Nora's behaviour and that the whole townland had laughed behind his back over the marriage deal that had fallen through, despite all his hard work.

'I am very disappointed in you,' he told her when she finally went to beg for his help. 'Of all my eight children, you are the cleverest and the one who could have achieved the most and you threw it all back in my face by marrying that ne'er-do-well. And look where that got you. You are on your own with six children and no one to help you to take care of them. Well, you have made your bed, my girl, and now you can lie in it, and you will be getting little sympathy from me.'

Since the early days of her marriage Nora had listened to this kind of criticism. At the beginning she had fought back, insisting that she loved Oliver and that he loved her and that all would be well between them. They just had to get settled in, she said, and then Oliver would start earning good money and everything would be fine. But as the years wore on, Nora had lost the will to argue and would simply listen to her father's angry reprimands in silence, twisting her hands in her lap. Her father still had the ability to make her feel like a small child as she sat in front of him listening to these furious tirades. Eventually she lost the gusto with which she had originally stood up for her husband, for she began to realise that Tom was on many counts correct. She also knew that no matter how Oliver behaved, it would never stop her father complaining.

*

It had always been Tom Langley's habit to get his own way by bullying and shouting, both at home and in his schoolroom. His temper was locally feared, but he was respected for his teaching abilities. In earlier years the pupils who graduated from his tutelage had obtained the highest scores in the primary exam that all children sat on reaching school-leaving age and, if their parents had not had to withdraw them to work on the family farm or in service, many would have been able to progress to secondary school and from there to university or into a profession. Although he may have used his temper to achieve this success rate, the fact that he always expected the best from them stood his students in good stead.

Tom's temper had worsened as his bitterness increased and, to make matters worse, he had begun to drink more than was good for him. Sadly, Nora's father had far more in common with Oliver than he liked to think. While it was true that he was an educated man, Tom was also a man of his culture and generation and vulnerable to the same temptations that drew in so many. He, too, was a familiar face at the public house and fond of having 'a few drops' at home in front of the fire or discreetly (although not as discreetly as he liked to think) behind his teacher's desk at work when the children were bent over their slates. As the years passed, he had begun to drink more and more heavily every evening, after he had been sipping from his flask all day. His bad temper was exacerbated by the alcohol and, although he was never violent, he could be very unpleasant in his tirades against life in general and anyone who had made him angry in particular.

He began to miss school and to rant at home about the cruel blows life had dealt him. 'What did I do to deserve this – a pack of ungrateful students and a daughter who has defied me all her life?' All those around him – and particularly his family – were targets for his anger. Gone was his pride in his work: alcoholism was ruling his life. In time these changes became even more evident in his classroom and he took his anger out on his pupils more and more frequently. Monday mornings were the times they dreaded his wrath the most – you could have heard a pin drop in the room as the children did their compositions or silently memorised a poem. In the afternoon his temper would improve – helped along by the little bottle of whiskey under the desk.

He resisted retiring long after it would have been wise to back out gracefully and his neighbours knew that it was just a matter of time before he was pushed from the position of which he had always been so very proud. There had already been many warnings that, unless his performance started to improve, he would have to go. But on his good days he could still be an excellent teacher and this was all that stood between Tom and a forced early retirement.

Finally the board of management at his small country school called Tom in for a meeting and told him that his teaching days were over. That if he went without making a fuss he could retire with dignity: everyone would pretend that nothing was amiss and that it was not his fault that his job, the source of all his pride, was being taken from him and given to somebody else. If he resisted, he would be sacked and would lose both his dignity and his pension rights.

'Is this the thanks I get for all my hard years of service?' Tom bellowed. But even to his own ears, his protests sounded hollow. They all knew that he could not teach any more.

This was a terrible time for Tom. Despite his protests to the contrary, he knew in his heart that he was no longer a good teacher. He knew he was not instructing his pupils properly and that alcohol was destroying him, both physically and mentally. He continued to hope in vain that he would be given a reprieve and kept on to work and finish at retirement age like all the other teachers. Eventually he had to concede defeat and realise that it would be better to accept retirement than to be forced out and humiliated in front of all his peers.

Despite the shadow cast on his departure, the school gave Tom a beautiful watch as a present on his leaving. Perhaps the members of the board felt sorry for him. In defiance of the local gossips who knew exactly why he had ceased to teach, Tom proudly hung the large-faced watch over the kitchen dresser, in full view of everyone who entered the house, as if to remind them that, whatever had happened and whatever foolish people might say to the contrary, he was an educated man who had done his best in very difficult circumstances. It would stay there in testimony to his many years of hard work and to his position as the most learned man in the community in which he lived.

*

All of Nora's siblings except for Mairead, the youngest, had left home. Josie, Maggie and Tom were in London and seemed happy in their marriages. Nora envied their easy rapport with her parents. There seemed to be no anger or disappointment driving *them* away from Tom and Ellen, nothing like the huge chasm that had opened up in *her* relationship with them. Even so, she had only to look at her own children to know that she owed it to them to bridge that gap. She was also aware that she could not continue to ask Nonnie for help, but must go to her own people. And so, although Tom had rejected her first pleas for assistance, she realised that she must keep on trying, even if that meant sitting through more angry lectures.

She was also clever enough to realise that one way in which she could gain a little help was by sending the grandchildren alone to visit with their grandparents. Tom and Ellen had no interest in visiting their daughter in

Templemore, but they did accept these visits from their grandchildren. This at least gave Nora a little time to herself and also meant that there were less mouths to feed at home, taking some of the pressure off her daily struggle to find enough food to put on every plate.

But Tom's grandchildren hated him because of his foul temper and lack of patience. The man who had once taken great pride in shaping young minds seemed almost to loathe his own grandchildren who, to him, represented his daughter's failures. As Nora's boys grew older, they began refusing to go to see their grandparents. But Kitty and Betty were always sent and they did not dare to refuse.

Their grandparents' cottage looked like fairyland, the children thought, with roses, peaches, plums and new potatoes all growing in the garden. The perfume from the roses was absolutely intoxicating in the evening. The inside of the house was fascinating too, full of little knick-knacks and fancies the likes of which the two little girls had never seen in their own home.

Kitty was particularly awestruck by the big face on the watch above the dresser. The watch stopped one day while she was admiring it and, in spite of all of her grandfather's efforts, it never worked again. Tom thought that Kitty was in some way responsible because she had been looking at it at the time. And so began his complaints about Kitty. He would tell his wife that the girl was possessed with noxious powers and that she was not an ordinary child, having caused his precious watch to stop just by staring at it. He said that she was a witch and that they would have to be careful around her because she might cast the evil eye on them.

Kitty was desperately upset by her grandfather's accusations. 'I never want to see my grandfather or his horrible watch again,' she sobbed against her mother's shoulder. But of course she had to see him; her mother sent her again and again to stay with her grandparents. Betty, although older, was even more terrified of her grandparents and, in consequence, was sent less often. In this case Kitty's greater courage was no blessing, as it meant that she had to suffer the torment of her grandparents' company more frequently. At least, Nora reasoned, there would be plenty of good food for Kitty to eat and she would be able to compensate for the meagre diet on offer at home.

Kitty's grandmother, Ellen, was a serious woman with a frown on her face at all times. In repose she looked sad but she did not talk about her sorrows, choosing instead to let them out in the form of rage. Ballycurran Cottage was always kept perfectly neat and tidy. Ellen worked hard to keep everything going, cleaning and polishing all day long. As she was getting older and had to spend ever more time taking care of her ailing husband, who was frequently the worse for wear as a result of the drink he had taken, this task was becoming more onerous. Whenever Kitty came to visit she put the little girl to work straight away, making her pay with her labour for the sins of her mother. Grandmother Ellen was quick to anger with the little girl and, in terror, Kitty worked as hard as she could. It was never hard enough for Ellen.

'Work never killed anyone,' Ellen would say to her granddaughter. 'And you are a young girl with plenty of energy to use up. We are feeding you very well here, so the least you can do is work for your keep so long as you are with us.' Kitty was sent to the pump three times a day for a bucket of water. The pump was a full mile away down the unsurfaced country road. By the time Kitty reached home, the bucket was invariably half-empty because it was too big a burden for such a small girl and it banged heavily against her thin calves, leaving great dark bruises, sloshing water out onto the road and soaking her socks and shoes. This, of course, enraged her grandmother, who would send Kitty straight back to fetch yet another bucket: 'And don't get your shoes and socks wet this time. I have more than enough to do without having to dry your things as well! A full bucket, this time, mind. What do I want with half a bucketful of water?'

To limit the need for water from the well, the family also collected rainwater from the roof of the house. It ran down a chute and into a barrel where it was stored for washing the floors and laundry, while the well water was used for cooking or boiling the kettle for a cup of tea. After fetching drinking water, Kitty's next job would be to wash the floors in the house, which was red tiles throughout. When the floors had been washed and had dried, paraffin oil was put on a cloth and all the tiles had to be polished to bring out the shine. Kitty was instructed that she should polish and polish again until she could see her own reflection in the tiles.

The fireplace was open, with bellows at each side that had to be squeezed repeatedly to start the turf burning. This, too, was Kitty's job. The fire burned turf and logs, with the sods having been harvested from the bog just outside Templemore. The Langleys spent long days in the summer digging out the turf and leaving it alongside the trench to dry out, hoping that the sun would shine for days on end so that it could be brought home in good time for the winter. Back at the cottage, together with the logs that were cut in the summer, the turf was left to dry out and then stacked neatly at the side of the house to be used in the long, dark months of winter. Stacking the turf and logs was Kitty's job as well. By the end of a day spent at her grandparents' house, the little girl only wanted to fall into bed and go to sleep. The food may have been more abundant and more nutritious than that available at home, but she paid dearly for it.

Mairead was dating a young man in the locality. One night she was going to a dance with her boyfriend and she found that she had no gown to wear, or at least none that she deemed pretty enough to show her young man. She sent Kitty, then fourteen, down to Cotchie Quigley's house to borrow a dress. Cotchie was her best friend and they shared whatever they had. The dress was a beautiful flaming red colour with a lovely flounced bodice, the height of fashion. But before Mairead could don the beautiful dress and start to put on her lipstick in readiness for the big night out, Grandmother Ellen found the garment, threw it on the fire, and blew the bellows so hard that the red cloth went up in flames while her daughter cried for the loss of the dress and because she knew that her friend was going to be very upset with her.

But Ellen was defiant and felt entirely justified in what she had done.

'No daughter of mine is going out in a whore's dress,' she said in response to her daughter's protests, 'and Cotchie's mother should go down on her knees and thank me for preventing her own child from going out dressed like that! That dress was an occasion of sin!'

Mairead went to the dance despite her mother's best efforts and told her niece to leave the bedroom window open, so that she could get in afterwards without waking her parents. Kitty spent the night waiting for Mairead's return. She was terrified that her grandmother would come into the bedroom and check for Mairead, only to find that she was not asleep in her bed but out at the dance with her friends and the boy she liked. Fortunately things went according to plan and there was no trouble.

A little while later Mairead had a date with the same boy. They had arranged to meet at the crossroads near her house. Kitty was brought along to keep watch in case their parents came looking for them both. Mairead gave Kitty a comic to read while she and her boyfriend had a kiss and a cuddle. Curious Kitty was more interested in watching the kiss and cuddle. Afterwards they slipped back into the house via the open window and no one was any the wiser about the illicit meeting. Secretly Kitty loved the excitement and the uncertainty of these rendezvous – would they be caught, or would they get away with it?

*

Although he was not yet very old, Tom was exhausted. He always had a bad chest infection that no amount of tonic would clear up and he coughed all day and night to the same chorus from his wife: 'Cough it up, cough it up, Tom Langley.' Sometimes when he coughed, it seemed extraordinary that he managed to survive the wracking spasms gripping his body every few minutes. Nobody wanted to admit it, but it was likely that he had contracted tuberculosis, a scourge that was sweeping across Ireland and claiming the lives of young and old.

He had been disgraced in the small community that was his home and his family bore the brunt of his loss of self-esteem; he continued to find solace in the consumption of alcohol and cigarettes in industrial quantities. He was so low that it now seemed nothing was off-bounds to him. In 1947 the *Nenagh Guardian* reported that Tom had stolen a consignment of cigarettes from a train at Thurles railway station and (after having hidden them for a week) had sold a number of them, telling his customer that he had purchased them in England.

He never helped his wife in the home. Ellen tried to keep out of her husband's way and to ignore his coughing and carrying on when he came home with 'drink on him'. His deteriorating condition only served to make her crosser and crosser, no matter how much she tried to avoid him. When the grandchildren arrived to visit she took her anger out on them. The only thing that he did do in his last years was to tend to his precious roses. Tom loved gardening and, whenever he was not in the local pub, he was in his beloved garden. His house was known far and wide for his roses and he even referred to it as Rose Cottage.

There was no change until one night, when Tom was seventy-two, Ellen woke to an unaccustomed silence in the room that they had shared for so many years and went over to check on her husband in his bed. Perhaps he needed her help? But Tom would never need anybody's help again.

Ellen did not sleep soundly again for the rest of her life – the awful silence in her bedroom kept her awake. Although her husband had been difficult and even violent at times, she found that she missed his coughing and heavy breathing – and even the loud snoring about which she had complained so often. In the morning, after a sleepless night, she would fall, exhausted, into a deep sleep and stay lost to the world until her daughter Mairead woke her for tea at eleven.

But after Tom's death Ellen and her children began to remember the good times. They remembered the proud village schoolteacher who had seemed to know everything about everything. They remembered seeing him out in the garden, content among his roses. Those moments, even in that last dreadful period of his existence, had always given them a glimpse of the father they preferred: the sober one, the one who cared about his flowers.

10

The wrong kind of match

By the time Kitty finished primary school, she had grown into a fine young woman, wise beyond her years and more than ready to move beyond her unhappy childhood in Templemore and on to bigger and better things. Although she was very bright and had always been a high achiever in the classroom, there was no question of her going on to further education as, quite simply, there was no money to support a grown girl in school. In 1940, when Kitty was fourteen, she found her first job working for a family in Dublin 4, an affluent suburb in the south of the city. Her employers, the FitzMaurices, had just two children, Elizabeth and Tommy.

Although she was still just a girl, Kitty did all the housework and cooking as well as looking after Elizabeth FitzMaurice, who came to be almost like a little sister. Tommy was older and well able to take care of himself. During the day she did all the shopping for the household in the upmarket butchers, bakeries and grocery shops of the surrounding neighbourhood. In fact the FitzMaurices left Kitty completely in charge and she soon acquired all the expertise of the professional housekeeper. She relished her responsibility.

Kitty and the FitzMaurices grew very close and she would remember them with great fondness for the rest of her life. George Fitzmaurice was a very wealthy man, the chief of the Bank of Ireland, and his wife was a very kind woman who held tea mornings and played a round of golf almost every day at the local golf club. She was ladies' captain on more than one occasion. They knew everyone in high society in Dublin and were well-liked and respected wherever they went. Elizabeth was sent to the best girls' school in Dublin to receive the finest education that money could buy. The contrast between Elizabeth's pampered childhood and the situation of the McManus children could not have been starker but Kitty never felt any resentment, just gratitude that her hard work was being rewarded and that she was treated with kindness and respect by her employers.

Kitty and Elizabeth gave each other pet names: Charlie and Fred. When Elizabeth grew old enough to start going out to the pictures, they went together, Kitty as excited as the younger girl to buy the tickets and the packet of sweets and to sit in the dark to watch the glamorous film stars on the screen. During her years with the FitzMaurices Kitty saw Elizabeth grow from a little girl into a fine, attractive young woman.

As she reached her twenties, Kitty began to think seriously about what she was going to do with the rest of her life. She had grown into a very good-looking lady, with the same fresh beauty that Nora had had as a young woman, and she was much sought after by the young men in her neighbourhood, even if her natural air of authority was a little overwhelming at times. More than once she had been accused of being bossy. But for the most part the Dublin men were very taken with her pretty looks and lovely figure and found her sense of humour, strength of character and independent streak very attractive. Though Kitty was friendly and chatty, she was always a little distant. Her coolness and distance intrigued her admirers, but the truth was that she was determined not to make a bad match or to let her heart rule her head – like her mother had done. She had seen first-hand what charming men were capable of and was not going to be fooled into the same mistake herself. If she had to wait a little longer, what did it matter?

'I am waiting for Mr Right to come along,' she would tell Elizabeth. 'I'll know him when I meet him. I'm saving myself for a good man.'

Kitty liked the bright lights of the city, but for the duration of her tenure with the FitzMaurices she still visited Templemore quite often and went out dancing with her old friends there. Despite everything Templemore still felt like home and Kitty felt that, when the time was right, she would return and settle down near her mother.

*

While Kitty was making her way in the 'big smoke', there were improvements in the fortunes of the McManuses back in Templemore. Betty now had a job that was similar to Kitty's, looking after a local business woman's household and her only child. And, like Kitty, she was lucky enough to make a good relationship with her employer; both girls would remain in contact with their first employers for the rest of their lives. Ollie had finally broken free of Templemore and the Brown family feud and emigrated to England, but he sent home a little money whenever he could. Johnny had taken over from Ollie in the local butchers' shop, working (as his brother had done before him) all hours that God made. It was Nora's great delight that she could look forward to the bits of meat and bones that he brought home every evening and then plan what to cook for the next evening's dinner.

Nora herself had found a little companionship in a new pet – a cat called Constantine, acquired not long after Kitty had moved to London. Kitty was now a very independent young woman, but whenever she visited home in Templemore, Nora would always tell her daughter that she had to be home at a certain time – and she enforced that rule. The same rule applied to the cat. Kitty would often hear her mother out on the street, long after she herself had gone to bed, calling Constantine to come home. Nora was more tolerant of Constantine's lapses, however, than she was of her daughters'.

On one occasion Kitty and Betty came in late from a dance, only for Betty to be greeted by a blow on the forehead from her mother's shoe. Blood was drawn and Betty went to bed weeping. She would bear that mark for many years to come. Most probably Nora was terrified that one of her daughters would be swept off her feet by some young buck and rush into a hasty marriage, just as had happened to her many years before. It is also possible that she had been drinking that night and had miscalculated her aim. For, in spite of Constantine's undoubted virtues as a companion, Nora's drinking had become a very serious cause for concern to her family. Whenever her older children came home from work on payday, Nora approached them with her hand extended.

'I need a bit of money from you for the housekeeping and to buy a bite to eat,' she would say. 'We all have to pay our way and, now that you are big, you will have to contribute to the household.'

Nora was making a fair point, however she increasingly used this money not for the basic necessities of life, but to drink herself into oblivion, the better to forget how very unhappy she was. She often went to the local pub on her own and sat in the snug, which was the only area where women were allowed. Nora always wore a shawl so that she could hide her glass bottle of Guinness under it, but she was deceiving herself if she thought that nobody knew that she was drinking. Her problem with alcohol was common knowledge in Templemore. Some people felt sorry for her, but others felt nothing but revulsion. Most men in Templemore drank to excess at times, but a drunken woman was seen as shameful.

Sometimes Nora brought her Guinness home and sat by the fire sipping it until she was drunk and had to be put to bed by one of her children. It was not hard to understand why Nora drank. This was a woman whose every hope had been dashed and who was now facing the prospect of spending old age alone. She was still only middle-aged, but she was officially married to Oliver and would remain so until he either turned up or was confirmed dead, and her difficult life precluded the possibility of forming another relationship. Aside from her love affair with alcohol Nora had few other pleasures in life. She took up smoking cigarettes, Woodbines and Sweet Aftons. Cigarettes soon became a passion and an additional drain on her scarce resources. Her children worried desperately about her. What would become of Nora as she grew old if she continued to drink as she did? And who would take care of her?

Nora's worst nightmare came true when her second youngest child, Seamus, caught tuberculosis in his late teens. Her family was nearly grown and things had been getting a little easier because several of the children were working and she no longer had to worry about how she was going to put food on the table all by herself. Although the sanatoria and hospitals were full of tuberculosis patients, so far the McManuses had escaped the scourge.

Seamus was a young adult when he became ill, working as a painter by day and playing music on his piano accordion at night. He had dreams of becoming an artist and had decorated the stairwell of Nora's small house with a beautifully executed ivy wreath. Now Seamus had to stop working and take to his bed. His lungs were badly affected by the disease and, after he failed to improve with bed rest, he was taken to hospital in Nenagh where the worst-affected lung was to be collapsed in the hope that the other lung would recover and proceed to do the work of two. The operation seemed to go well, but afterwards Seamus deteriorated very quickly and it was discovered that the surgeon had collapsed his good lung in error.

To everyone's shock, Seamus died shortly after the botched operation, without ever coming home from the hospital. Most of the town came to his funeral, as he had been a lively soul whose music had delighted anyone who listened to it.

Nora never recovered from Seamus' death. She had already been a broken woman, but now all the light faded from her eyes and there was no joy in her life.

*

Elizabeth Fitzmaurice had now grown up and was working in a bank, just like her father. With every educational and family advantage it would not take Elizabeth long to make her way up through the ranks and eventually she would become one of the first female bank managers in the country.

As for Kitty, now in her late twenties, she felt that it was time she started to think about marriage before the years passed and she found herself on the shelf. Although she was still a great beauty, she worried that she was already getting too old to find a mate and she knew that she had probably held out long enough for the right man. Most of the girls she had gone to school with were already married with several children. She joked that she was waiting to meet Orson Wells, her favourite actor and ideal man. 'If he only came to Dublin and saw me, it would be love at first sight!'

How Kitty longed to find a man she loved to settle down and raise a family with. She was also concerned about her mother, who had aged suddenly after Seamus' tragic death. She made the decision to go back to Tipperary because she knew that she wanted to be close to home with her own people and in a place she could be herself, somewhere she felt comfortable. But it was a huge decision, for it meant that she had chosen against Dublin and settling down with a Dublin man. Kitty was aware that her choice in Tipperary would be more limited. It seemed that most of the young, attractive and successful men had already been snaffled. But Kitty was determined and sure that she was destined to meet the right man for her in her home county.

And so, with good wishes and many hugs, Kitty left the FitzMaurices for the last time and went back to Templemore. From that day onwards Elizabeth and Kitty kept in constant contact, exchanging a letter or a phone call every week.

It took Kitty some time to settle back into life in Templemore, which seemed very staid and quiet after the bright lights of the city. Of her brothers and sisters, only Richard remained in the town. While life had not been easy for any of the children, perhaps it had been least difficult for Richard because he had never really known his father, so he had no memory to grieve over.

Richard had been musical ever since his childhood in the Christian Brothers, having inherited Nora's fine singing voice. As an adult he had formed his own jazz band and played the saxophone at weddings, in pubs and at dances. Richard loved to recite poetry to his mother or anyone else who would listen and his favourite was 'Lucy Gray' by Wordsworth, a sad poem about a little girl who died in a storm. Richard liked to tell the story of how, one night when he and two friends were returning home after a night of playing at a dance, one of them had shouted: 'Why did he send her out that night in the snow? He *knew* the storm was coming. The bastard!'

Because Richard recited the poem so often, everyone knew straight away what was being referred to.

Richard had married Vickie, a beautiful local girl with long auburn hair that she wore off her face and up in a twirl on her head. They were looking forward to starting a family. Everyone but her, it seemed to Kitty, was happily paired off and anticipating a future by the side of someone they loved. What did life have in store for her?

Apparently what destiny had in mind for Kitty was a rather dour widower called Dessie Green, a man decidedly lacking in the personal charm that most women find attractive. Dessie, who had also grown up in Templemore, was a successful local builder. Kitty lived in terror of returning to the poverty that had marked her childhood and knew that she could never settle down with a poor man. There were many who still struggled to make a living in Ireland in the late 1950s, but Dessie earned good money and, being a few years older than Kitty, seemed to offer a stable family home. Kitty was in her early thirties by the time she married and was considered a spinster because women married very young in those days. Dessie was about thirty-six and already a widower. Kitty was never ashamed that she was interested in the financial security that Dessie could offer; she knew that her future husband was neither handsome nor exciting, but she knew that he would look after her properly. Her mother had married for love, and look what that had brought her. With Dessie she would never have to suffer the poverty and insecurity that had ruined her mother's life. After a troubled childhood, Kitty was sure that she had found her safe mooring.

In Templemore some people said, unkindly, that Kitty was a gold-digger who was marrying Dessie for his money. This may have been partly true but it was a two-way marriage of convenience. Dessie had been looking for someone to take care of his motherless family, having had to send his daughters, Bernadette and Mary, to live with the nuns in the absence of a woman in the home. Fathers were not expected to take on the role of single parent in those days. Dessie's first wife, Jane, had been ill for a long time before her death. He had been under tremendous strain keeping his business together, minding the girls and caring for his sick wife. It had also been hard for the daughters; they had tried their best during their mother's illness to help her and to keep the house tidy for their father, with a little help from kind neighbours. When all was said and done, it was a great relief to Dessie's friends and family when he remarried, since they knew how much he needed a wife. They also felt that Kitty would be the perfect wife for him, especially since she was already in her thirties and had worked away from home as a housekeeper in Dublin. She was smart and wise and knew about life; she would be a good companion and take care of the lonely widower's house very well. Most importantly, the girls would be able to return from the orphanage and enjoy a proper home life again.

And Dessie loved Kitty, at least at first, in spite of his undemonstrative ways. He was very proud of having found such a pretty and clever wife for himself. 'You'll be my equal partner in everything,' he reassured her. 'I know that your mother had a hard time, but you can trust me. I love you. I would never do anything to hurt you.' Kitty had found herself a kind man, with hidden depths and the soul of an artist. To this day, everyone in Templemore knows one of Dessie's works: a great steel cross erected on the Devil's Bit Mountain near the site of the miraculous well of James Welsh, overlooking the town. Dessie had made the huge monument first in wood and then in steel. It can be seen shining for miles on a sunny day.

But Nora was not pleased. She thought that Kitty might be better off not marrying at all and told her that people often didn't turn out as they first appeared. However, she stopped short of warning Kitty not to marry Dessie; no one knew better than she that love was no guarantee of a successful relationship and that it was important for Kitty to have a comfortable lifestyle. There were others who thought that Kitty, with her good looks and quick wit and her contacts through the FitzMaurices, could have done much better for herself. Kitty listened to nobody. She had made her own mind up and was determined that she knew what was best for herself.

Kitty and Dessie were married quietly in the parish church in the presence of their friends and relatives. The wedding breakfast and reception were held at home in Nora's house. Betty and Nora had organised everything for the meal after the church; a wonderful feast of the sort that had never been seen in the house before. Nora could not stop rubbing her eyes and exclaiming at the sheer quantity of food and drink on offer.

The night before the wedding Betty, Kitty and Nora cooked all the meat and prepared all the vegetables. They made chicken soup and baked brown bread. They polished the glasses until they shone. Kitty carefully hung her beautiful wedding dress outside the wardrobe, ready with her shoes and bag. Before going to bed, she put in her rollers and slept in them all night to have her hair looking well for the big day ahead. She was satisfied that she had been very organised and that she had done everything she could to ensure a grand beginning to her life with Dessie.

On the day of the wedding the guests feasted on turkey and ham, with a glass of wine to toast the bride and groom. Nora had baked a beautiful three-tier wedding cake and decorated it with a statue of a bride and groom at the top. She had had the local baker ice it, with icing flowers bordering each layer.

Everyone enjoyed the day and evening, until Kitty found Nora sitting in a corner with a glass of porter in her hand, looking very much the worse for wear.

'Mammy,' Kitty called. 'What are you doing?'

Nora opened one eye wide and glared at her daughter. 'I am enjoying myself at your wedding.'

'How many glasses of porter have you had?'

'Not too many.'

But Kitty could see that her mother had had more than a few. In fact she was drunk and incapable of carrying on a conversation with anyone. Embarrassed, Kitty called Betty and, between them, they took Nora upstairs to her bed, where she stayed for the remainder of the night.

Nora was keeping something back from Kitty. In a sense she could not even admit to herself the shadow that she had seen; she was frightened of the truth, a terrible truth that might ruin everything. She certainly did not want to discuss it with her strong daughter Kitty, who had always been able to look after herself. For Nora had suddenly remembered those old rumours about a Mrs Green and her safe house. Now she could hardly bear to look at her lovely daughter on her wedding day and imagine the terrible mistake that Kitty might be making. And yet, she comforted herself, she had always had her own doubts about that vicious gossip. So she had decided to keep the dark worries to herself. Instead she had become very drunk.

Downstairs the men of the family and their friends took out their instruments and played dance music, swing and jazz. In the small kitchen the table and chairs were pushed against the wall so that the revellers could dance. To the shouts of their friends, Kitty and Dessie were the first on the dance floor. They made a handsome couple, she with her dark, tossing curls and he, tall and distinguished and so proud of his new bride. The music and dancing went on until the sun rose, whereupon the party spilled out into the front garden and onto the street. The neighbours gathered to hear the music and wish Kitty and Dessie well. It seemed as though the whole town was there. Word had spread quickly about the wedding in the McManus house.

*

After the festivities Kitty went to live with Dessie in his comfortable house on the outskirts of town. She forgave Nora for her embarrassing behaviour at the wedding and they visited each other often, becoming closer than they had ever been before.

Neither Kitty nor Dessie knew about the gossip that circulated around Templemore and Nora never spoke of the feeling of dread that had suddenly overcome her on their wedding day. But there were many others in Templemore who recalled that, back in the days of the Black and Tans, it had been Oliver McManus sleeping with Mrs Green, Dessie's mother, when she became pregnant. Everyone had known it; hadn't Oliver boasted about it in the pub? Hadn't he said that she was 'an old one, but a good one.' Hadn't they all known that Mrs Green's husband had been too elderly and too decrepit to get his wife in the family way? About nine months after Oliver's boasts, Dessie had been born. Five years later, Kitty had been born. Could it be that Kitty McManus had married her own half-brother? Could that *really* be true? Nobody could prove it, but it seemed more than likely to more than a few of the local gossip mongers.

The newly-weds were happy enough, settling into their new lives together. When Dessie came home every evening, the first thing he did was to hold Kitty's face in both hands and kiss her on the lips.

'What did I do,' he would say, 'to deserve to come home every night to a woman like you?'

'It must have been something very good,' Kitty would tease.

Kitty set high standards for Dessie and, in the beginning, he was willing to go along with her way of doing things. She kept her home spotless and ran it as she had run the FitzMaurices' in Dublin. She bought all the latest household gadgets and at first Dessie never baulked at paying for them. Kitty's garden was immaculate and she ensured that there were always some flowers blooming, whatever the season. On entering the house, guests always felt very welcome. The hallway was decorated with landscape paintings that Dessie, a talented painter, had done himself and there was a hall stand with a long mirror in the centre, coat hooks on either side, and a place for umbrellas. The floor was paved with stylish green, cream and wine-coloured mosaic tiles that Dessie had put down, with a circular design in the centre. Their home was envied by the neighbours and Kitty worked very hard to keep it looking beautiful all the time.

Dessie's daughters, Bernadette and Mary, were eleven and thirteen when Kitty married their father. They had spent two years in the orphanage. Twice Kitty had visited them there in the days just before her marriage. She had explained what was to happen and that she hoped to be a good mother to them when they were back under their father's roof. They were clearly shocked and unhappy that their dad was taking another woman. They already knew of Kitty and knew that she was looked up to in Templemore, but they were a little daunted by her bossiness. None of this could stop them longing to be home again. When they finally arrived there, it was not at all the same: their mammy was gone and Kitty ruled the roost. The house itself had changed completely because their new stepmother would not rest until she had everything she wanted. The neighbours thought that Kitty was kindness itself to take in the two motherless little girls.

At first Kitty did all their cooking and cleaning and washed and ironed their clothes, hoping that her hard work on the girls' behalf would make them fond of her. But very soon she could see that Bernadette and Mary were too old to accept her as a mother substitute and she lost patience. The way in which they idealised their real mother, whom they still missed desperately, irritated Kitty beyond belief. Soon it was obvious to everyone that there was no love lost between Kitty and her stepdaughters. Years later Kitty would freely admit that she had been cold and even cruel at times to the motherless girls. She had resented their standoffishness and done little to court their affection, gradually demanding that they did more and more of the housework until they were doing almost everything. Many years would pass before Kitty managed to build a good relationship with her stepdaughters.

Kitty and Dessie had just one child together, a little girl they called Monica, who was born a couple of years after their marriage. She was a delightful child, and Kitty was very proud of her and doted on her from the moment she arrived. She made a wonderful mother and it was a great comfort to her to know that Monica would never have to do without, as she had.

But Kitty's relationship with Dessie began to deteriorate even before Monica was born. Although he was quite rich, Dessie was also rather tight-fisted and had grown used to being on his own. Soon he was asking Kitty to account for every penny that was spent and to justify everything she did. Kitty, who had also spent so much of her adult life on her own, did not appreciate being told what to do, or being advised that she would be better off buying a cheaper shampoo, or repairing her stockings instead of buying new ones. They started to argue, so loudly that the neighbours could not help but hear.

The rift that was opening between Dessie and Kitty went far deeper than arguments about money, however. By now the rumour that she had married her own half-brother had reached Kitty's ears. She had been in the pub one evening when a drunken old man came up and told her, laughing, that everyone knew her father had slept with Dessie's mother, and that it was popular opinion that she and her talented husband were in fact half-brother and sister.

'And what do you think of that, young lady?' he had asked her drunkenly.

Kitty said nothing. She stared at him for a long minute and then turned on her heel and left, her face white and still.

Kitty's affection for Dessie vanished overnight when she realised, in horror, that the rumours might be true. She knew about her father's philandering ways; everybody did. She had heard that he would sleep with any woman who made herself available to him. She had been told that he had had children all over Templemore, raised by men who were not their fathers. She had seen photographs of her mother-in-law, dead these long years. Mrs Green had been a very attractive woman, even in later life. Oliver would not have turned down an opportunity to go to bed with her. The bastard! Not content with ruining her childhood and that of her siblings, Oliver's carelessness and lack of regard for anyone but himself was destroying Kitty's life in adulthood, too.

Kitty tried to put the old man's poisonous words out of her mind, but she could not. They came back to her, over and over again, and began to torment her every waking moment. She became obsessed with the fear that everyone in the town knew about the dirty rumour and was staring at her whenever she left the sanctuary of her own four walls. What was the whole of Templemore saying?

Then she began to wake in the night and to stare at Dessie as he slept, fancying that she could see a family likeness to herself. Dessie, too, had heard the rumours, and bitterly regretted that they had not come to his attention before the marriage had taken place. But they never voiced their fears out loud to each other. Their unspoken secret became a burden they each had to carry about every day. Nothing could be proven and nobody would ever know the truth of the matter, but the secret was there, festering between them like an infected wound. A wound that grew and grew until it eventually it would wreck their marriage.

Kitty spoke to none of her family about it. She wasn't sure if they had heard the rumours as well – if they had heard anything, they never mentioned it. She was too shocked and ashamed to ask them, but she suspected that her mother had heard the filthy prattle. She even guessed that her mother had known before the wedding but had kept in her mouth shut to protect Kitty. Kitty could only pray that her daughter and stepdaughters would hear nothing. It was something that played on her mind for the rest of her life.

Gradually Dessie and Kitty grew apart until they might as well have been two strangers living together. In the meantime Kitty had discovered that she had the gift of being able to tell fortunes and the rumour spread around Templemore that she was a sort of witch, with powers that went far beyond the ordinary. People were intimidated by Kitty and her flashing eyes, but they still went to her house to have her read their tea leaves and tell them what their futures held. While most fortune-tellers churned out the same promises of marriage and children, Kitty's visions of the future could be disturbingly accurate. Kitty would make her guest a cup of tea and, when she had drunk it all, ask her to swirl the cup around and then turn it upside down on the palm of her hand. The leaves that remained behind told the fortune, which could be good, bad or indifferent.

Young and old alike loved to get a reading done. Mostly they wanted to know if they would find love, or if the fellow they liked at a distance would somehow figure out that they had a crush on him. Kitty was impatient with such timid women. In her day she had never been too shy to approach the men she liked and had always been prepared to suffer the consequences if the man did not wish to date her. There were many surprises, but Kitty's readings invariably came true. So much so that more and more people started referring to her as a witch, at which point she gave up the habit because she did not like the name or the reputation that went with it.

'I didn't like it when my own grandfather called me a witch when I was a child,' Kitty said. 'And I don't like it now, either.'

One of the last readings Kitty did foretold a terrible event for the person in question and, when it came to pass, Kitty was desperately upset and swore that she would never dabble with the supernatural again. She sought solace in the fact that she had never told the person of the tragedy that lay ahead and that at least she had not had to worry about it before it happened.

She also thought to herself that it was ironic: here she was with the gift of seeing into others' futures – how could she have known so little about the man she had married? But then, if she had not married Dessie, she would not have had her beautiful, perfect daughter, whom she loved so very much. Whatever the truth of Dessie's parentage, there was absolutely nothing wrong with Monica. Kitty promised herself that she would always, always shield Monica from the awful truth that her mother and father were half-brother and sister, no matter the cost. In her heart of hearts, she knew that there was no saving her marriage, not even for her daughter's sake. This was a dark time for Kitty and it affected her ability to cope with life and her behaviour towards those she loved.

*

The final instalment of Kitty's marriage to Dessie played out while she was visiting her sister Betty near Kilkenny. Betty had met her husband, Noel, in Templemore when he was a soldier at the barracks, with duties as a radio and Morse code worker. It was a whirlwind romance and they had married when Betty was just nineteen and Noel twenty. A year into their marriage, while they were still living at home with Nora, the first of their five children, Walter, was born. Another three children would follow, with a final surprise baby girl when Betty was in her forties and her youngest was already eight.

A few months after the last baby was born Betty was taken ill and had to go into hospital, so Kitty went over to take care of her children. They were quite frightened about their mother's illness and about who would look after them if she took a turn for the worse. Insensitive to their fears, Kitty set about rearranging the furniture in their house until it no longer looked like their home. The children were behaving as best they could under the circumstances, nevertheless Kitty was always telling them to sit still, be quiet and not to move, and she was full of complaints about the way in which they had been reared. Nor did she keep her ideas to herself, but aired them to everyone prepared to listen.

'They have no manners on them at all,' she moaned frequently to Betty's neighbours. 'It's as well that I am here to teach them how to behave while their mother is away.'

Kilkenny city was the nearest big town and Betty had always done her weekly shop there. While Kitty was caring for the children she enjoyed going into town and soon knew all the shopkeepers. One day she took her niece Marie shopping and embarrassed the little girl when she stopped at a greengrocer's to enquire about the availability of the purple tissue paper in which the oranges were wrapped.

'Is there any chance I could have a bit of that?' Kitty asked loudly. 'You see, my sister Betty has no toilet paper in the house, just bits of old newspaper, and that purple stuff looks as though it would be much softer on my bum.'

The bemused greengrocer handed her some of the paper as Marie blushed because she felt that the world would know they had no toilet paper at home. Kitty was totally unaware that she had mortified her niece, she was just after something for free and damn the rest of them.

Soon Betty was home again, much to her children's relief. But while she was convalescing Kitty stayed on in the house and kept Monica with her. Kitty's little girl was growing into a spoilt child, being her father's youngest and her mother's only child. During that visit with Betty she was always given what she wanted and taken everywhere with Betty and Kitty, while Betty's children stayed at home, angry and tearful about this favouritism. Even when Monica misbehaved, stabbing one of her little cousins with a pencil and leaving a wound, she was not chastised. She was the apple of her mother's eye and could do no wrong.

And then, one evening when the children were playing in front of Betty's house in their quiet country road outside the city, a powerful big lorry pulled up in front of it. The children stood and stared in awe, never having seen a lorry so close before. In fact there was hardly any traffic at all on that little road.

'Give Monica to me,' a man shouted from the cab of the lorry. 'I'm taking her home.'

The driver's door swung open. The lorry looked huge, dark and menacing. Dessie was inside, red-faced and terrifying.

Kitty had seen what was happening from the house and she ran out into the road now. 'Monica is not going anywhere,' she shouted. 'She is staying right here with me, and you can feck off.'

She grabbed Monica's arm. Dessie jumped down from the lorry and grabbed the other arm and the two started to pull as Monica's cousins began to cry, afraid that the little girl would be torn in half by the two furious adults. The petrified children ran back into the house and urged their parents to stop the row. Betty and Noel were very cautious and knew that Dessie would back off, which he did.

Eventually Dessie conceded defeat and left, but this was one of the last times that Kitty and he were together in the company of her family. Everyone could see that their relationship had deteriorated to the point at which it could no longer be repaired. The events of that night forced Kitty's hand and she left his house for good, returning to her childhood home with Nora, who was now elderly. With no income, she knew that times would be hard again, but she had no intention of remaining in a difficult situation. Now that she was on her own again, she was determined to get a good job and pay her own way.

She would put her failed relationship behind her and start a fresh chapter. It was a brave decision for a woman from a land in which divorce was unthinkable. But Kitty had seen her mother tied for life to a man who had abandoned her, and she realised that she needed a clean break in a new place, away from malicious gossips and rumour. She felt that she would have to leave the country.

11

Foreign shores

It was 1962 when Kitty decided to move to England and find work, sure that she would do much better there than she ever could in Templemore. There were many more options for men and women who were not afraid of hard work and Kitty had always been very happy to roll up her sleeves and get on with things. Kitty left three-year-old Monica with Betty for three months while she searched for a job and an apartment in Leicester. During those months she lodged in the home of a widow called Doris, who had several lodgers and lived on the proceeds of their rent. She was a kind older lady and she and Kitty were soon firm friends. On one of her first evenings there, Kitty had looked at Doris long and hard.

'You are still a very good-looking woman,' she told her. 'But why don't you put on a bit of make-up and put a rinse in your hair? And dress up a bit. You look very dull.'

Astonished by Kitty's bluntness, Doris just stared back at her. But she let Kitty do up her face and before long she started to accompany her out in the evenings and at the weekends.

As soon as she had found a job and a home for Monica, Kitty packed her bags and got ready to leave for Ireland, telling Doris that she would always be welcome to visit: 'I've a feeling we're going to be friends for a long time yet!'

Monica had managed reasonably well with her young cousins in Ireland. There was a big age difference between the girls but, because she was an only child and very self-contained, she was used to playing on her own. She often seemed to be talking to herself and when she was asked what she was doing, she would answer simply, 'Oh, I'm talking to my two friends, Phac-phac and Thie-thii.' Her cousin Marie became fascinated with this game and Monica was delighted to involve her. Phac-phac and Thie-thii came to bed with Monica and Marie, they got up with them and had dinner with them. Monica spoke to them so clearly that Marie was sure that they were real, but that there was something wrong with her and this was why she could see nothing. Eventually Betty told Marie about imaginary friends, but the little girl still suspected that Phac-phac and Thie-thii were real for a long time. Finally she was convinced that they definitely did not exist and she was quite devastated because they had become part of her life too.

When Kitty came back to collect Monica, she looked very different: younger, and very sophisticated, with a new hair style, glamorous make-up and an independent air. She was almost unrecognisable as the stressed, tired woman who had taken her leave just a few months before. Kitty stayed for a few days and then left with Monica and, of course, Phac-phac and Thie-thii. Marie missed them all when they left, including the imaginary friends.

Kitty was so determined to start a new life in England that she even adopted a new name, 'Cathy', which is another diminutive for Kathleen, her official Christian name. All her new friends knew her as Cathy, although her family in Templemore could never really accept it and insisted on calling her Kitty. She found a job as a home help, which was hard work but reasonably well paid. Monica went to nursery school locally and they settled into normal life in an ordinary English suburb.

Dessie and his daughters had also arrived in England by this time, settling not far from Kitty's new home in Leicester. He and Kitty met each other there and briefly tried to rekindle their relationship far away from the wagging tongues of Templemore, but it was not to be. As they were living in England, it was at least possible for them to get a divorce, draw a line under their failed marriage, and move forward with their lives. Their reconciliation and amicable divorce brought a bonus for their children. Bernadette and Mary loved their little sister Monica and, now that they lived close by, they often babysat her and took her out. Kitty was delighted that they all got on and was grateful that the girls helped her with Monica.

Once she had settled down in Leicester, the FitzMaurice family were the first people to visit Kitty. They had always maintained contact and were anxious to know how she was faring on her own, and whether she needed any help. They told Kitty that they would always be there for her and that she should visit them at their home in Dublin whenever she returned to Ireland. Kitty promised to do exactly that, never dreaming that she would be the one to offer help, rather than to receive it.

Not long after their visit, Elizabeth FitzMaurice rang Kitty to tell her that she had a terrible problem: although she was not married, she was expecting a baby. This was a dreadful situation to be in, especially for an ambitious young woman such as Elizabeth. Without a moment's hesitation Kitty invited Elizabeth to stay with her in Leicester until the baby was born, so that she would be safe from prying eyes and would have some time to think about what she wanted to do. Elizabeth could not tell Kitty who the baby's father was, but hinted that he was much older, well known, and married. Elizabeth did as Kitty suggested, the baby girl was born and, with great sorrow, Elizabeth gave her up for adoption and returned to Ireland. For years to come Kitty would receive calls from Elizabeth in the middle of the night, always distraught about her baby girl.

'Where do you think my baby might be?' Elizabeth would sob.

Kitty always did her best to reassure Elizabeth. 'I bet you anything that she has the best home in England. I know that she is going to have a wonderful life. Don't worry.'

'It's so hard,' Elizabeth would say. 'I know I chose to give her up and signed all the papers, but I can't stop thinking about her. I want to know where she is.'

'Sure, you'll get married and have another baby,' Kitty always told Elizabeth. 'That won't replace your daughter, but it will help.'

Sadly, Elizabeth never did have another child. In later years she found a partner and concentrated on her very successful banking career instead. But she never forgot about her baby girl, continuing to hope that she was loved and cherished in her new home and would have a happy, successful life. She regretted that she had not written a letter for her, telling her that she had loved her but could not mind her due to circumstances. If Elizabeth had done so, then her adoptive parents would have been able to give this sign of love to Elizabeth's daughter when she was eighteen. Instead, she could only pray the child would understand when she became an adult herself.

*

The McManus children had scattered by now, but some stayed in contact with Nora more than others. While Kitty was in England organising her new life, her brother Ollie went back to Templemore for a visit. In effect Ollie had turned his back on Ireland and this would be his only trip home in many years. In England he was doing very well as a successful roofer, but his partner in life, Ethel, had seen some hard times. She had been married before and had not been divorced at the time she married Ollie. When this was discovered by the authorities, Ethel was prosecuted for bigamy and served time in prison. Nora had been proud to see the difference between Ollie's behaviour and that of his father's, for during this difficult time Ollie continued to stand by his commitment to his partner and to care for their little girl, Anita, while he waited for Ethel to serve out her sentence.

When Ethel was finally released, the time was ripe for a visit back to see his mother, whom he greatly missed. Ollie arrived on his motorbike, accompanied by some of his biking friends and with Ethel travelling in his side-car. First they visited Nora and the other Templemore relatives, then headed on out to Betty's house in the countryside near Kilkenny. The bikes caused great excitement because they were never seen in Ireland in those days. Sound travelled for miles and country people's ears were attuned to the noises of their roads: because the roar of the engines was so much louder than any car, no one knew what to expect before Ollie and his friends appeared. Wherever they went, children came out to see what the commotion was and to chase the little cavalcade down the road in great glee.

Betty was so excited to see her brother that she laid out a great spread and invited all the neighbours to come and see the guests and their fine motorbikes. Ollie impressed his little nieces and nephews with his navy pin-stripe suit, his black leather coat and the goggles over his eyes, and Ethel cut a dash in a black and grey hound's-tooth coat that reached down to her toes, black leather gloves and a woollen cap.

When it was time for Ollie to leave, he told his mother and Betty that he and his family were preparing to leave for Australia. There was employment for all skilled workers out there and he felt that the hot climate might alleviate his asthma. Since he was such a good roofer, he had been offered free passage and the promise of work on arrival. This was goodbye. He was not planning to return to Ireland to live ever again, and it was unlikely that he would even visit.

Nora wept bitter tears at the thought of parting from Ollie for the last time and, as usual, sought solace in her Guinness and cigarettes. Nora was easily moved to tears and had cried just as abundantly when her first grandchild, Walter, had been born. Then she had wept when Betty moved to Limerick after Noel's battalion was transferred. She wept again when they returned to Kilkenny – and she continued to weep every time they came to visit.

'Why are you crying, Mammy?' Betty would ask, half touched and half exasperated.

'Your children are so beautiful,' Nora would sob. 'And I love them so much. It makes me sorry I could never enjoy your childhoods, as I was always so busy and worried.'

Now she wept because she knew that she would never see her beloved son again.

*

Back in Leicester, Kitty, who had been such a poor stepmother to Bernadette and Mary when she was married to their father, was now starting to become quite an important figure in her stepdaughters' lives. The girls were teenagers, young adults, and they appreciated having a mature woman close by, someone to whom they could go for a little female support and counsel. They had started dating and, without a mother of their own, often came to Kitty for advice about the men they were going out with. They were not intending to marry young, but planned to have fun for years before they settled down. And so they did.

Bernadette in particular led quite the high life, at one point she would even date a singer who later became famous as Engelbert Humperdinck, although at the time he was known by his birth name, Arnold George Dorcey. In years to come, Kitty would often remind her family of Bernadette's claim to fame. She was especially pleased because she was a fan of Engelbert's songs 'Release me', 'There goes my everything' and 'The last waltz'.

Talking to Bernadette and Mary about their exciting young lives reminded Kitty of when she herself had been in her twenties and working in Dublin. She reminisced about her dancing days and the big ballrooms with the fantastic floors where she had glided with her tall, handsome partners: 'Ah! There was nothing like it!'

Kitty was particularly pleased that Bernadette and Mary adored Monica and were always good big sisters to her. The girls loved to spoil the little girl, taking her shopping and buying clothes for her. As result Monica, even at the age of five, was already turning into a young lady who was very particular about her appearance. Children's clothes and shoes were very expensive but Kitty gave in to her whims, remembering how she herself had been teased by the other children at school for wearing worn old clothes. Sometimes Kitty would tell Bernadette and Mary that she felt as if she were reliving her own childhood through Monica – but this time in the way it should have been.

Kitty's pretty young niece Mary (Betty's oldest daughter) came to live with her aunt and look for work in England. Mary had been working in a shop in Kilkenny but she had earned very little money and there was little prospect of obtaining anything better. The emigration from Ireland continued unabated throughout the 1960s and Mary knew that her ambitions to get on in life and do well could be better realised overseas than at home. But it was very hard on her family – they knew that when people left they very rarely came back.

Kitty was very supportive of her niece and Mary found work in a dressmaking factory, where she quickly became very skilled. In return for all their help Mary made beautiful dresses for Kitty and Monica. She often sent a parcel of clothes home to Ireland for her mother and the children as well; everyone in the little house in Kilkenny would wait with great anticipation for the postman to cycle up on his pushbike and deliver the package. She planned the clothes for the people she loved carefully, buying the material cheaply at the market in Leicester and thinking carefully about the colour and style that would suit each of her younger siblings, who rejoiced in the fact that they were the best dressed children in the church at Sunday Mass.

After she had been living in England for only a short time, Mary already had many admirers and soon met the young man that she would marry. Mary's beloved was a handsome Tipperary man who was also living and working in Leicestershire. They often laughed about how they had had to travel all the way to England to meet each other. Their meeting had been pure chance, given a little help from a persistent Mary. She had seen him leaving the house opposite Kitty's when she was on her way out to work one day and she had liked the look of him. Although she was shy and reluctant to appear too forward, she studied his comings and goings to make sure that she would bump into him regularly; soon they were saying 'good morning' to each other. Tommy was shy too, but eventually he plucked up the courage to ask her out and in no time they were meeting once or twice a week, usually to go to a dance or to the pub. Women had not gone to pubs in earlier years but now most girls accompanied their boyfriends, although Mary always had a glass of juice. Tommy enjoyed a pint of beer with his friends.

When Mary came home from her dates, Kitty would ask her to tell everything. Mary would blush but oblige with a few details. Although Kitty knew that Tommy was a very sensible young man, she was anxious if Mary stayed out late and told her that she should always come home early. She felt responsible for Mary's welfare and, knowing how hard Mary worked between her job at the clothes factory and the shop job that she had at the weekends to earn money to go home for her holidays, she felt that the girl should be getting plenty of rest.

Mary lived with Kitty and Monica until she and Tommy were married. Always the talented seamstress, she made her own wedding dress, as well as dresses for her bridesmaid (her sister Marie) and her flower girl (her sister Carmel, Betty's youngest). Mary's gown was of white satin, with a long train attached to a satin belt at the waist. She wore a pill-box hat of fine lace, with a short veil flowing from her headband. Her dark brown hair was backcombed high on her head and turned under at the nape of her neck. In hands that were covered in white lace gloves to match those of her bridesmaid and flower girl, she carried a bouquet of red roses with a trail of maidenhair fern, just like her Grandmother Nora had, entwined with white satin ribbon for dramatic effect.

It was 1964 and Mary wore heavy pan-stick makeup, powder, blusher, eye-shadow and many coats of thick, black mascara. Mary's twelve-year-old sister Marie was tremendously excited to wear her emerald-green, full-length satin dress, with a pill-box hat made from the same fine lace as the bride's. Her hair was dressed in the same style and she even carried a matching bouquet. Carmel, who was still just a little girl, wore a beautiful dress of gold satin in the same design as the bridesmaid's dress, with white shoes and a lace headdress. The colours had been chosen to add a patriotic accent on the day: green, white and gold. Because Mary was living in England, she had had to ask her sisters to take their own measurements and send them back to her by post. They did as instructed, but Marie dreaded the thought of gaining or losing a pound for fear the dress would not fit. When the day came, it fitted perfectly.

*

And then Nora, old before her time in her mid-sixties, became ill and needed to be taken care of. Nora was fonder of her Guinness than ever, although she insisted that she drank it for medicinal purposes only. Having heard from Betty that Nora was not well, Kitty went to Ireland to see her mother. She was shocked by her decline and Kitty and Betty both agreed that Nora could no longer live on her own. None of Nora's other children were in a position to care for her because they all had large families, and so Kitty decided that the best thing would be to take her over to England to live with her. When Kitty explained to her mother that she wanted her to come back to Leicester, Nora was devastated.

'I'll be alright here in Templemore,' Nora insisted. 'Sure I have Richard and Vickie right here to call on me and check to see if I am alive and kicking.'

It took a lot of persuasion on Kitty's part to convince Nora that she needed to be taken care of and that she could not live alone anymore. Several weeks passed before Nora would even consider the idea, although Kitty asked her siblings to help talk their mother round. And then came a night when she had one too many falls after drinking; it shook her, and she was persuaded that her life in Templemore was no longer what it had been. Even so, she continued to plead her case.

'But I was there before I married your father,' she said, mournfully. 'I know it was in another city, but isn't England all the same? What's the point of me going back now, after all these years?'

'A lot of time has passed,' Kitty told her mother. 'England has changed a lot, especially Leicester. I'll take you to the Corn Exchange where all the big dances are held. It's just off the market square and it's one of the biggest dance halls in England. During the day we can go in and have a cup of tea and a bun.'

'Well,' Nora grumbled. 'I won't be going to any dances in that whatever-you-call-it place.'

'Ah no, Mammy. I didn't mean for you to go dancing. I was just explaining what it is like. Sure you could have the cup of tea and the bun when you are in town with me on my day off every Saturday?'

'I won't eat any dirty English buns there at all. I'll get my own when I come home. I don't want everyone looking at me drinking tea and eating buns. You know I don't have many teeth left in my mouth now. Anyhow, I don't know anyone there to be talking to. I would have to sit on my own in a place where I know no one.'

'I have my own house and there's a grand big room in it for you, with space for all your books and bits and pieces. You'll be at home there, wait and see.'

'Will you let me hang up my picture of your father?'

'I will, of course,' said Kitty, through gritted teeth. 'If that's what you want.'

'I don't know. I will miss Templemore and all my friends.'

'What friends, Mammy? Sure, you are here on your own most of the time, with nobody to talk to. You will grow to love England again and we will have a good life together. And you can help me too; you'll be able to look after Monica when she gets home from school every day. We live near the city centre and we can go and have a look around the shops when I am off on a Saturday. I'll introduce you to my friends. They all know about you already and are dying to meet you.'

'But what will I do with all my furniture here in this house? I don't want to throw out perfectly good furniture. Anything I have I want to keep. It's not much, but it means a lot to me.'

'Mammy, believe me, this furniture has seen its day. There is nothing you need from here, Mammy, we have all you need. You'll have a more comfortable house to live in and you'll be with us.'

Eventually, after much enticing, Nora agreed to move. There were many goodbyes and many tears were shed before she left. With each farewell, Nora drank several bottles of Guinness and smoked innumerable cigarettes. When the day to leave finally came, Nora and Kitty left the little house and closed the front door for the last time. Nora turned around and looked over her shoulder.

'Look forward, Mammy, not back,' Kitty urged. 'We're in this together and it's for your own good.'

There were tears in Nora's eyes as she climbed into a neighbour's car to be driven to the train to catch the ferry in Dublin and she buried her face in her hands while all the families on the street waved her goodbye as she set off to start her new life with Kitty.

As the train pulled out of Templemore, Nora turned to Kitty with a question: 'Did you arrange to have my post forwarded to me? Your father might be wanting to send me a letter in England.'

Although Nora had been in England as a young girl and had done very well there, she found it almost impossible to settle down in Kitty's house in Leicester. Perhaps being back in England reminded her of the opportunities she had thrown away many years before. Kitty did her best to make her mother feel happy and welcome in her new home, but Nora soon became bitterly depressed and spent most of the day indoors with the curtains half-drawn, refusing to go anywhere or see anyone. She found it hard to understand the local accent and could only be persuaded to leave the house when Kitty took her to visit friends. Finally Kitty invited her old friend and landlady Doris over for tea. Doris made a huge effort to be kind to Nora and her efforts paid off: Nora even went to Doris' home to return the visit. But afterwards she said that Doris was probably the only nice person in Leicester and renewed her complaints.

Nora had become terrified of almost everything. She was scared of buses. She was scared of bridges. She was scared of her own shadow. She often created a scene when she and Kitty were out in public, insisting that something bad was going to happen and that they were both on the verge of being seriously hurt or even killed.

Kitty grew exceedingly exasperated at Nora's behaviour in public: 'Stop embarrassing me,' she would hiss. 'Nothing is going to happen to you, for feck's sake. Stop drawing attention to yourself. Stop making a show of us.'

'I want to go back to Templemore,' Nora would say miserably. 'At least there I know where I am and I feel safe.'

'Well, you can't go back to Templemore and, with you drinking all the time, it's not safe for you to live on your own. You are not going anywhere and you know it. You will just have to make the best of it.'

Indeed it was a wonder that Nora had managed to get by so long without setting the house alight, as she often fell drunkenly asleep in front of the fire with a cigarette dangling from her mouth. But she would not even try to make the best of it. Instead, she seemed to be determined to be miserable. The strange thing was that, frightened as Nora seemed to be, when Kitty and Monica were out of the house, she was very well able to get across the busy road where they lived and go into the pub for a pint bottle of porter.

When she had first arrived in England, Nora had started drinking her porter in the afternoon. As it did not take much to go to her head, by the time Kitty came home from work Nora was quite drunk. She was very slight and she ate almost nothing, appearing to subsist mostly on alcohol. Then she started drinking in the morning, going across the busy road as soon as the pub opened its doors. She drank her pint directly from the bottle and was tipsy by lunchtime. Sometimes when Monica came home for lunch she would find Nora drinking out of the bottle.

'What are you doing, Granny?' Monica would say. She would take the drink and pour it down the sink and then check Nora's purse to make sure she did not have money for more porter. Monica was sure that she was doing the right thing for Nora, but sometimes Kitty privately thought that, considering the number of disappointments and betrayals Nora had suffered in the course of her life, perhaps it would have been kinder to let her have her porter, as it seemed to be the only thing that gave her any pleasure now.

All of Nora's beauty was long gone and nobody would have recognised her from her wedding photographs. Her hair, which she wore to just below her ears, was as white as snow. She had just one or two teeth left, one of which was a big bottom tooth at the front of her mouth that she would stick out to cover her top lip when she was feeling cantankerous, which, increasingly, was most of the time.

All day long Nora would sit in her armchair, poring over her books with the one eye that still worked well enough to read. She held the book close to her face and worked her feet, as though she were walking. Because she was alone in the house for most of the day, she could sit and read all she liked and pop out to the library whenever she wanted another book. Soon she started to combine these trips to the library with trips to the pub for another bottle of Guinness, or maybe two. She sipped her Guinness as she read, and maintained herself in a steady state of inebriation.

When Kitty came home from work (she still had a job as a home help for the elderly and disabled) and Monica came home from school, Nora was usually angry and rude to them. All her inhibitions were destroyed by the amount of alcohol she had consumed during the day. She criticised what they were wearing, what they did, and who they saw. She seemed to have nothing good to say about anyone now.

'Stop it, Mammy,' Kitty would shout, putting her hands over her ears during one of Nora's regular tirades. 'If you don't have something nice to say, don't say anything.'

But nothing would stop Nora. For most of her life she had kept her feelings inside, suppressing everything she wanted to say. That was just not going to happen anymore.

'This food is rubbish,' she would say to Kitty, pushing away her plate so violently that it almost fell off the table. 'The food in Ireland is better. This stuff is not fit to be eaten. This is like dog food. In fact, I wouldn't even give it to an animal.' She grew very thin.

'Turn off that television,' she would shout, if someone was watching something, or 'Turn that on! What are you waiting for, you lazy lump?' when it was time for her own programme.

'I won't have that rubbish on that you like to watch,' she told Monica. '*My* programme is much better.'

It was not always easy to be patient with Nora and the stress of being with her constantly took its toll on her daughter. One day Nora told Kitty she wanted to be buried in Ireland when she died.

'Well, you may as well start walking now,' Kitty said wearily, 'as I can't afford to send you back to Ireland for burial.'

Nora and Kitty did their best to get along in their respective ways, but it grew progressively more difficult for them to live together, and there were many arguments. Every night Kitty put her mother to bed with a hot water bottle to warm her feet, hoping to have an hour's respite in front of the fire with her book or the television.

'Come up to the bedroom,' Nora would shout, moments later. 'There's a cat in the bottom of the bed. Get that dirty cat out of here. I won't have a cat in my bed!'

'Well now,' Kitty would have to say, once again. 'What is wrong with you? Don't you know it's the hot water bottle, not a cat?'

'I wouldn't have minded if it had been Constantine,' Nora would complain. 'He was a fine, clean cat. But who knows where those dirty English cats have been?'

Ten minutes later there was always another problem. It was the same every night until Nora finally fell into a drunken sleep.

It was painfully difficult for Kitty to see her mother self-destruct. She did her very best, although she was often exasperated with her. She cooked the meals that Nora liked and tried to make sure that she ate them. Left to her own devices, Kitty knew that her mother would eat nothing at all.

*

As she grew older, Kitty surrounded herself with young people and adored the excitement of getting ready to go out. She threw herself into the pleasure of dressing up, doing her hair, painting her nails, plucking her eyebrows and putting on her eye-shadow. Often she would ask Monica or one of her nieces to help with her make-up, determined to look her best even for a trip to the local pub.

Whenever Kitty went back to visit the family near Kilkenny, she liked to visit a public house that was favoured by Betty's family and owned by a close relative. Ensconced in the snug, Kitty always ordered a Guinness for herself and a glass of orangeade for her niece Marie, who often accompanied her. One day Kitty daringly went into the public bar where the men drank. The barstools were all full and the men sat drinking, smoking and talking among themselves. They all looked up to see who was coming in.

'Hello!' said Kitty brightly. 'Terribly sorry to disturb you. I'm looking for Al. Al Capone. Has Al been in today? Have any of you gentlemen seen him?'

'No, missus,' one man said. 'I don't know any Al. I don't think he comes in here.' He consulted with the other men sitting at the bar, but none of them had heard of anyone called Al either.

'Well now,' Kitty remarked to her niece as they returned to the snug. 'They don't know very much, if they don't know who Al Capone is!'

Marie held her sides with laughter and the next time Kitty took her to the pub she made her do the same trick again – and again the time after that. How had Kitty ever come up with such an idea in the first place?

On another evening Kitty had been drinking several Guinnesses in the self-same snug, in company with a crowd of men and women. Suddenly she decided to up and tell them that she was a professional conductor from Chicago, the Windy City. Somehow she persuaded them all to pretend that they were playing musical instruments: some were given imaginary violins, while others had saxophones, trumpets, drums, a cello or a guitar.

Everyone 'played' their pretend instruments with great enthusiasm and vigour while Kitty conducted. When Kitty decided that the moment was right, she pointed her baton at whoever she wanted to 'play'. Each instrument had its turn and then, with both arms aloft, Kitty indicated that they were all to play together. Having no inhibitions, she did not care in the slightest if someone wandered into the snug, saw the silent orchestra playing its heart out, and thought he or she had walked into an asylum. Everyone in the house that night sang and did a party piece for Kitty. For years afterwards the customers of that pub eagerly enquired as to when Kitty would be over on her holidays again. Her zest for life had touched them all.

On yet another wild night Kitty left the pub where she had been drinking with her nieces and found herself in a supermarket car park filled with shopping trolleys.

'I've had the best idea!' she said. 'Put me in a trolley and give me a spin!'

For about an hour Kitty was wheeled around as she shouted, 'Come on girls, push faster! We don't have lift-off yet.'

On one of Betty and Marie's visits to Leicester, they accompanied Kitty to a local pub, the Blue Moon. The darts team was short a player and Kitty leapt up to volunteer her efforts.

'We're serious about our darts here,' one of the men said, rather dubiously. Everyone was surprised when Kitty, who had never played darts before, beat even the best of the seasoned players. Nobody was more surprised than Kitty, who was delighted and celebrated with several rounds of drinks. When they all arrived home, Kitty ordered Marie onto the balcony of her house, telling her that she should sing an Irish rebel song at the top of her voice. Marie did as she was told, although she was embarrassed to see the neighbours' curtains twitching.

'Can I stop now?' she begged after the first song. 'The neighbours are all awake.'

'Good enough for them!' Kitty retorted. 'At least now they know that we are Irish here!'

It seemed that Kitty, as a mature woman, was doing her level best to make up for many unhappy childhood years.

12

The quest

Kitty, still very attractive in middle age, had started dating again after spending several years on her own. Feeling guilty about leaving Nora alone in the evenings, she decided that her mother would be happier if she had some friends of her own age. Kitty herself had no trouble finding male companionship – she had simple tastes and enjoyed having a drink in the pub – but Nora had become a complete recluse and it was hard to see how she would ever meet anyone. If Nora had a friend to go out with, Kitty was sure that she would be happier and more settled.

She set about getting someone for her mother with her usual determination. The postman was very friendly, so Kitty introduced him to Nora. Nora had a habit of staying in bed, so the postman would come and sit on the end of the bed to keep her company while Kitty went out for a drink or a meal with one of the men she had met in Leicester. Nora was not impressed with this arrangement. She always sat as far away from her guest as possible and made herself as unattractive as she could for fear that he would touch her. She had never trusted men since Oliver had abandoned her and, although the postman was a decent, attractive gentleman of a similar age, she found his presence repulsive and decided that she would never be friendly with any man at all.

Whatever the company Kitty tried to organise for Nora, her mother remained distant and refused to play along. However the fact that Kitty was daring to go out and enjoy herself at all seemed to annoy Nora more; she was always particularly difficult to handle when Kitty was dolling herself up in preparation for a night out.

'Where do you think you are going?' she would mutter. 'Who are you going out with? Be careful what you get yourself into, because men are not always what they seem.'

And, although Kitty was now into her forties, Nora would stay awake waiting for her to come home from her dates and then accost her when she heard the key in the lock.

'What time of the night do you think this is to be coming in at?' she would shout. 'You have to get up for work early in the morning! This is disgraceful behaviour, young lady!'

Kitty had grown used to Nora's rages and she shook them off.

'Go back to sleep, Mammy,' she would say. 'Don't stay awake until this time of night on my behalf. I'll worry about myself in the morning. I'm a grown woman and I don't need you minding me the way you used to.'

The worst of it was that Nora seemed to know she was approaching death and began to talk about Oliver again.

'I just wish,' she would often say, 'that I knew if my Oliver was still living or if he has gone to his heavenly home. I think that I have stopped believing in God, because if there was a God out there surely he would show me a sign or give me a word to put my mind at rest. If I knew that Oliver was gone, it would somehow make it easier for me, because I would know that my husband would be there waiting for me.'

Nora seemed to be less angry with Oliver now. She had begun to remember how deeply in love they had been in the early days of their relationship.

'Wouldn't it be grand,' Nora would continue, 'if, when I die, I meet him at those pearly gates and he shows me the path to walk down, just as he showed me all the lovely places to walk in Manchester? How would he greet me after all that has happened throughout our lives?' This time he will only have time for me, he won't be able to go to foreign places for work, he will be so content in his heavenly reward. When I go over to the other side his smiling face will be there, "waiting, just waiting for me". We will have so much to talk about, so many memories and so much joy to share. It will be even better than the time we first met in Manchester, as it will be so peaceful. I will have him all to myself with no distractions from anyone. It will be just the two of us, like it was when we were so much in love.'

This was hard to listen to, to know that, in spite of everything, Nora still loved Oliver. Nobody could understand how she could, but this was all that Nora would say now about the man who had left her. All her life Nora had never spoken badly of Oliver; she had always said that she would never give up her search for him and that, if necessary, she was prepared to move the sun, moon and stars to find her husband, the father of her children.

When Nora died in 1968 at the age of sixty-eight, she was a shadow of the woman she had once been.

Weakened by years of malnutrition and drinking to excess, she slipped into a coma one night and never awoke. Nora's funeral was attended by her family, who spread her ashes in a beautiful rose garden near the crematorium. Nora had lived a hard and difficult life and had spent most of it simply longing for her husband to come home. Her children thought of their brother Seamus and knew Nora would have thought of him, too, before she died.

Nora had been such a strong personality that Kitty's home seemed eerily quiet without her mother ranting, raving, moaning and complaining. Kitty missed her, but was glad her mother had found peace and hoped she was with Seamus. She thought of her father and how his reckless nature and immaturity had destroyed Nora's health and confidence. She wondered if he was still alive or if he had gone before his wife. Strangely, she had a feeling that Nora's husband was still out there somewhere – probably breaking someone else's heart, or drinking someone else's booze. Kitty knew that wherever her father was, he was most likely causing trouble.

*

In the late 1960s Kitty's life finally began to blossom a little. She was already in her early forties and had spent many years working as a home help when she was lucky enough to find a lighter, happier job in the local post office as a clerk. The postmaster was about fifteen years older than herself, a widower with two grown-up sons whose wife had passed away years before.

Arthur was a real gentleman. Soon Kitty fell for his quiet good manners and his gentle ways. He opened doors for her, pulled out her seat at the restaurant, and picked up whatever she let fall. They started to see each other romantically and decided to marry, despite the fact that Arthur's two adult sons, who had families of their own, were opposed to the match, fearing that they would lose out on their inheritance. As Arthur was well-to-do, Kitty was moving up in the world. She had always had to work very hard for every luxury and she was pleased that the man she had fallen in love with would be able to provide her with a comfortable home.

Theirs was a quiet wedding in the heart of the city of Leicester. Arthur was distinguished in his dark suit and dickey bow and Kitty was still beautiful with her coal-black hair in a short perm. She wore a deep purple, stylish two-piece suit with a white blouse and a small headdress of purple mesh gathered together with a purple rose. The mesh fell down either side of her forehead and framed her beautiful face. She held a simple bouquet of deep pink roses with some maidenhair fern. Ten-year-old Monica was her bridesmaid and was dressed in a short, matching, purple satin dress. They both wore purple shoes that Kitty had had especially made to go with the outfits they were wearing.

After the ceremony the bride and groom and their handful of guests retired to a very exclusive hotel in a village just outside the city; Arthur had arranged everything, with no expense or time spared. A red carpet awaited them when the chauffeur-driven car pulled up outside. A champagne reception followed and then the wedding breakfast was served to the guests. It was a delicious meal with an extensive wine list chosen by Arthur. He himself did not drink, but in former years he had learned a great deal about wine.

The night before the wedding Arthur had sent a fantastic display of flowers to Kitty's home, with a note telling her how much he loved her and looked forward to spending the rest of his life with her. Now he leaned over to whisper in Kitty's ear.

'Is everything alright, my dear?' he asked. 'I wanted it all to be perfect for you.'

'Well,' Kitty answered, 'I'm sorry that my friend Doris died recently and couldn't come but, as you aren't capable of raising the dead, I have to say that it's as close to perfect as it could possibly be!'

'I haven't forgotten anything?'

'Nothing at all.'

All Kitty had to do was sit back and be beautiful, which came very easily to her.

After the reception Arthur and Kitty went for a honeymoon in Blackpool. On Arthur's arm Kitty felt that she could truly relax for the first time in her life. Finally she was with a perfect gentleman who looked after her, made her feel special and loved her deeply for who and what she was. Most of all, he was not from the home town that she loved and hated in equal measure. He knew nothing of the dirty rumours about her relationship to Dessie and had felt only sorrow for her when she told him about her father's abandonment of his family.

This was a real clean slate; Kitty had started a new life with someone who was from an entirely different place and, what was more, she could be quite certain that she and her new husband were not related. She could not have been more proud, excited and happy when she took Arthur back for a brief post-wedding trip to Ireland and the whole of the extended family seemed to approve. It was the icing on her wedding cake.

In Leicester Kitty now delighted in being the postmistress and the wife of a well-to-do man who had several houses in the city. Even her daughter was delighted for her and seemed to recognise that her mother had, at last, found a man who deserved her. Life was finally good.

*

Kitty had had a secret mission all her life, but she had not been able to embark on it until now. She had nurtured this dream since childhood. Kitty wanted to find her father, Oliver, and make him answer for the terrible things that he had done to her family and for how dreadfully they had all suffered as a result of his neglect. Now that she was with Arthur perhaps it would be possible, although it would call for considerable organisation and quite a lot of money. The McManuses were scattered in all directions – Canada, America and Australia. Kitty did not even know if her grandparents were still alive, although it seemed unlikely. If Oliver was still alive he would be an old man. But she was sure he must have taken excellent care of himself and felt that there was a chance that she might find him.

All that Kitty knew was that she should start looking for her father in North America – but it was a very big place. How and where should she start? The prospect of hunting someone down in such difficult circumstances would have been daunting for anyone but Kitty. Kitty considered hiring a private detective, but in the end she decided that nobody could do the job of searching for him better than herself. With nothing to go on and no leads, Kitty and Arthur decided to start their search in Chicago. It was a random choice, but they knew the city was a popular destination for Irish emigrants and there was something about the very name on the map that seemed to pull them there, even although Kitty's last

McManus contact address had been Canadian. And so, leaving eleven-year-old Monica in Dessie's care, they set off to track down their man.

It was October when Arthur and Kitty arrived in Chicago and just beginning to get cold. While they recovered from jet leg, Kitty examined the telephone directories provided by the hotel and discovered that there were still people by the name of McManus in Ottawa, the last location that Nora had had for Oliver's parents. Ottawa was only a short distance from Chicago, so she booked a flight immediately. As soon as they arrived, she rang the numbers she had found. These contacts turned out to be her aunts and uncles. Kitty and Arthur couldn't believe their luck. It was as if fate had intervened on their part. Kitty's relatives were delighted to hear from her. When she asked them why they had never contacted Nora and her family, or sent them money and clothes, she heard a terrible explanation. Her relatives had been told that Nora did not care about her children and had put them into an orphanage to be raised by nuns. They had also been told that she lived alone and was able to survive on her own, requiring no help from them, and that there was no way of contacting the children, who were being taken care of by the authorities.

'Who could have told you that?' Kitty was about to ask when, suddenly, she realised that the story could only have originated with one person: Oliver. Probably he had told his sisters and brothers what he wished was the case, absolving himself of guilt in his own eyes. Perhaps he had even come to believe in this horrible story. Even so, Kitty privately wondered why his parents and siblings were not concerned for their daughter- and sister-in-law, knowing how difficult it had been in Ireland before they all left for America and Canada. But, because her long-lost relatives were so welcoming, she put these thoughts out of her mind.

Kitty and Arthur were shown all the sights and Kitty enjoyed the big family parties that were thrown every night, although she did not lose sight of her main purpose. She asked everyone she met if they knew anything about Oliver's whereabouts and if they knew whether he was dead or alive. Nobody seemed to have any information at all. They all repeated that the last they had heard from him was when he went to Ireland to bring his family to North America. After that, they insisted, they had never heard from him again. He had completely disappeared in 1932. They had reported him missing and at one stage had even had the Canadian Mounted Police searching for him. All avenues had been exhausted and everyone felt it was likely that Oliver had died.

'Well, he's missing for sure, then,' Kitty said glumly. 'Don't the Mounties always get their men?'

This was very bad news and, to make matters more difficult, Kitty and Arthur could not stay in North America indefinitely; they had to return to Leicester and look after the post office. But something told Kitty that she was not being given the full story.

*

When Kitty returned to England, she took some time to reflect on her trip. She recalled all the conversations she had had with her aunts and uncles about Oliver. Something didn't add up. Afraid that she was getting carried away, she discussed her concerns with Arthur.

'I think you're right,' Arthur said after some deliberation. 'There is something they're not telling us.'

'Yes. I'm sure that they would know if he was dead.'

Kitty's instincts were correct. Uncle Jack, the youngest of all the uncles, rang Kitty late one night.

'You know,' he said. 'I think that Oliver just might be in Chicago. Maybe, if you contact the Mayor of Chicago, Mayor Daley, he will be able to help you find him. I've a feeling that he's not dead at all. I've a feeling that you just might be able to find him if you look in the right places.'

Kitty and Arthur booked a flight back to Chicago and set about arranging a meeting with the mayor. Kitty being the sort of person who would stop at nothing to get what she wanted, this was soon achieved. The mayor turned out to be very helpful and accommodating. He told Kitty that he knew where an Oliver McManus lived, but was not at all sure if this was the one in question. However, on Kitty's insistence and after some more research, he was able to tell her that this was indeed the man she was looking for.

Almost forty years after he had abandoned his family, Oliver's whereabouts were known! What a revelation. Could this be really her father? Kitty had been determined to find him, but a small part of her had always doubted that this was possible. She could not wait to get to the address she had been given and Arthur had to step in and slow her down. It turned out that Oliver McManus had married again and had a second family in Chicago. What shocked Kitty more was when she discovered that the oldest child had been born in the same year that her father had returned to Ireland. The year he had had his children vaccinated and arranged passports for them. By that stage he had already met another woman and she was pregnant.

Here, at last, was the real reason he had never sent money back to them. Kitty could not believe it. Despite all the years that she had spent apart from her father, it had never occurred to her that he might have found another woman and married again. It added a whole new element to her quest. First she had thought that he was dead. Then she had heard that he was alive. Now she knew where he lived, but she had to consider the impact that her visit would have on his second wife and two children.

After reflecting for a few days, Kitty decided to ring her father. The feelings of Oliver's new wife and children were not her problem.

Silence greeted her on the phone when she finally made the life-changing call. Finally Oliver's shocked voice came back down the line to her. His tone made Kitty wonder if, on some level, he had expected that one day he would be found. As he spoke, Kitty pondered what he looked like now. Was he still striking, with a twinkle in his eye? Was he standing or sitting? What was the expression on his face like? Had he lost his breath? Was his heart racing? Had he broken out in a cold sweat?

I hope he's had the worst shock of his life, she thought fiercely. That's the way I want him. Afraid.

This was the moment she had been building up to for decades. The gloves were off now, and Kitty was going to hurt him. She had been rehearsing this moment, this first contact, for most of her life. Had he often wondered what had happened to his wife and six children back in Ireland? Had he expected that one of his children from Ireland would eventually find him? Had he ever considered how selfish he had been to abandon his family in order to start a comfortable new life for himself?

Kitty did not know how she felt. As a child she had loved Oliver, which had made his betrayal even worse. Now she thought that perhaps she hated him, but she still wanted to see him for herself. Something told her that she would never be completely at ease until she had met him face-to-face and set some old ghosts to rest.

'You can come over if you want,' Oliver finally said. 'You can come tomorrow.'

Kitty put down the telephone. Did she want to go at all? Now that she was so close to her goal, she was no longer sure that she still wanted to see her father. She felt nervous and needed a drink to steady her nerves. She tried to recall the last time she had seen him. She remembered how happy she had been when he returned from the States and got them passports. But then she recalled all the years of torment. She thought of Nora. She thought of her siblings. She decided she would go at least for them.

'You know I will support you in whatever you decide,' Arthur told Kitty, squeezing her hand.

'I know.'

The night before she was due to see her father, Kitty could not sleep. She tossed and turned in her comfortable hotel bed until morning. She did not know what she wanted to say or how she would react, although she had anticipated this meeting for so long. All she wanted was to stand in front of him . . . or did she? Would she even recognise him? She could barely remember what he looked like and she had been a child when they had all waved him goodbye. How would he react when she arrived? Would he be angry? Sad? Did he feel guilty? Did he feel *anything*? And what about his new wife, if wife indeed she was? How was she going to react? Then a thought struck Kitty. Perhaps his two children would be there. Now *that* was something that she had not been prepared for. Perhaps they did not even know that they had a whole family of half-siblings in Ireland. Perhaps they would be furious. Perhaps there would be an ugly scene.

In the morning Kitty paced while she waited for the taxi to arrive. She had decided that she would ask the taxi to take her to the nearest Catholic church before going anywhere. She wanted to kneel and pray for her mother and light a candle. She wanted to ask God to shine his heavenly light on Nora today and, somehow, to let her know what Kitty was about to do after all these years. She would be closer to Nora in a church, with her lit candle shining towards Heaven.

Kitty sat in the chapel and thought of Nora, remembering her during her last days on earth. She had spoken about Oliver a great deal.

Mammy should be here in Chicago herself, she thought. She should be the one to confront him.

'If there is a God up there,' Kitty whispered, 'please let my mother know what is about to unfold today. Please give me some sign that she knows where I am and who I am going to meet.'

Kitty rose to her feet. She genuflected to the altar, bowed her head respectfully and left the chapel.

'Come on now, Kitty,' she said aloud. 'You can do it.'

At the bottom of the steps up to the chapel door, Kitty saw a white feather lying on the tiles. She stopped, bent down and picked it up. This was the sign that she had been waiting for.

'Thank you, God,' Kitty said, looking towards Heaven. 'Now I know that you are with me, and Mammy too.' She picked the feather up and put it into her handbag.

Back in the taxi, Kitty put her hand in Arthur's. Arthur looked at Kitty with sympathy and concern.

'Now I feel better,' she whispered.

Kitty had not told her sister and brothers about her plan to see their father. She did not know how they would react. They were all married and had children of their own and most of them had moved on with their own lives – all but Seamus, who had died so young. But surely they were all still angry with the man who had left them when they needed him most, when they were hungry and thirsty? They had grown up seeing their mother transformed from a beautiful, gifted young woman to a woman old before her time, lined and worn and exhausted with the effort of raising six children on her own in a society that did little to help women like her. Abandoned and unable to divorce, Nora had never had the opportunity to start another relationship without being branded an immoral woman. Kitty could remember seeing her mother waiting, endlessly waiting, year after year, for a telegram, a phone call or anything to let her know what had happened to the man who had once seemed to love her so much. She had written to her parents-in-law, but they had ignored her. She had reached out for help, but she had been turned away.

Kitty wondered for a moment why she had even bothered contacting the McManuses. What sort of people were they, abandoning their own family to the hard times that they themselves were escaping? Years had passed, and they had never contacted their daughter-in-law and grandchildren. How could they have done such a terrible thing? Had they no conscience? Even when Oliver remarried, nobody had written to Nora to tell her what had happened. Kitty was sure, now, that the stories she had heard in Canada about Oliver's disappearance were not true. She knew that the McManuses had known of Oliver's whereabouts all along. They had all simply chosen to forget Nora and her family, at home in Templemore, because they did not care. Nobody had cared.

Kitty and Arthur climbed into the taxi. It drove quickly through the streets of Chicago but Kitty could see nothing, lost in thought as she was. Finally the yellow cab came to a halt and Kitty was jolted out of her reverie.

'Madam, we have arrived at your destination. That will be four dollars, please.'

'Keep the change,' Kitty said slightly awkwardly as she handed over five dollars. She was not used to giving tips, as was customary in the States.

Kitty stood on the pavement and looked up at the tall, grey apartment building she was about to enter. It was the afternoon and the sun was shining from a lovely blue sky. She shielded her eyes to look up at the windows, wondering if her father was looking down at her.

'Will you wait in the foyer?' she asked Arthur. 'This is something I need to do by myself.'

'Of course.'

Kitty went to the clerk behind the desk.

'I need to get to number 537, please.'

'Yes, Ma'am. The lift is across the hall.'

13

Confronting the past

Slowly and carefully Kitty walked towards the elevator, her handbag dangling from her arm, both hands clasped in front of her. She had dressed carefully and was wearing her navy suit with a white blouse and navy shoes to match her suit and bag. Her black hair was in the latest style. Her eyes looked tired, as she had slept badly the night before, but as the excitement and adrenaline kicked in, she started to move more quickly.

Well now, she thought. This is it, come on, Kitty. This is the moment you've been dreaming of all these years.

The building was clean and seemed to be new, and the elevator smelled faintly of disinfectant as Kitty travelled to the fifth floor. Her heart was beating fast as she reached the door. She rang the bell. A few uneasy moments passed.

Come on, Kitty thought. Open up and let me in.

The door opened to reveal a woman in late middle age. The woman stared at her silently and then walked away, leaving the door open.

Is that the old hag my father is with all these years? Kitty thought viciously. Jesus, just look at her. She is not a patch on our mother, Nora. Is this what he has lived with all this time? She must have something I don't see. What was he thinking? Kitty felt like slapping her, but she knew not to waste her energy on the woman. She wanted to save her energy for the man who most deserved it. The man that had married her mother and left her with six children to fend for herself.

Kitty walked down the short corridor to the main room of the apartment, where she found herself standing before a gaunt, miserable old man in a wheelchair who was sitting and staring straight ahead. She could see that he had spilled soup on himself earlier and that he was wearing an incontinence nappy beneath his grey trousers.

Kitty assessed her feelings and determined that she felt nothing. She did not shake her father's hand. He was a complete stranger to her. He looked nothing like she had imagined. Much as she may have pictured this moment for years, right back into childhood, he had never looked like this.

'I'm Kitty,' she said. 'Your daughter.'

'Don't start shouting and carrying on,' Oliver said. 'The neighbours will hear you.'

'I don't give a shit who hears me!'

Oliver stared at Kitty in silence as she looked around the room. There was a heavy mahogany sideboard covered with bowling trophies.

'Are they yours?' Kitty asked, nodding at the trophies.

'Yes,' Oliver said weakly. 'I won all of those for bowling.'

'Well now,' Kitty replied. 'While you were off bowling, did you ever wonder about your family in Templemore? Did you ever ask yourself if we were dead or alive?'

Oliver said nothing.

'The least you could do is answer me. Are you going to say anything, or are you just going to sit there?'

Oliver's rheumy eyes filled with tears that spilled over and ran down his cheeks. But still he said nothing. Kitty stared at her father and made no attempt to comfort him.

She wasn't sure if he was crying crocodile tears, or if they were tears of regret. Did he feel remorse, guilt, shame, or did he just feel sorry for himself? Kitty longed to know what he really thought and how he really felt, but she was too furious to ask. Though she was almost shaking with emotion, something inside her felt cold as she watched him crying. She couldn't help thinking that there was something pathetic about him crying and not saying anything. She even felt it was an excuse to say nothing.

'How is Betty?' Oliver finally asked.

'She's very well,' Kitty replied. 'She got along fine without a father. She did very well for herself and married a good man who takes care of her. She has five children and they are all fine too.'

Silence again.

'Did you ever think about your wife, Nora, as she is the only wife you have ever had? You were married in the Roman Catholic Church and you did not get divorced, so the woman you are with now is not your wife. You're a bigamist, and so is she. And whatever children you have are bastards.'

Silence.

'You destroyed my mother,' Kitty said. 'Only God knows how we all coped and came out alive. Only God knows how we managed not to die of hunger or disease.'

Oliver said nothing.

'You bastard,' Kitty screamed, suddenly losing control of her feelings. 'Is that all you have to say to me after all these years?'

There was no reply.

'Your second youngest son, Seamus, died of TB.'

Kitty waited for a response but none came.

'Your wife, Nora, my mother, died two years ago. She loved you unconditionally even though you left her when she was young and needed you most. She had six children for you, six children who would have died for each other. Throughout their childhoods and beyond, they were everything to each other and gave each other all the support that you denied them. They all wanted and hoped that you would come home and return to the family. You know, every night we all got down on our knees with Mammy and prayed fervently and earnestly for you to come home. Throughout our childhoods we were hungry and cold without a father to comfort us and be there for us. Those were the years when we needed you most. We felt all the emotions: sorrow, hatred, love and longing. Most of all, we wanted to be wanted by our father. Did you know that we often blamed ourselves for the fact that you were not there? We thought that we had done something wrong, something that made you leave us. At other times we blamed our mother, Nora, for the situation we found ourselves in. We blamed our country and the troubles in Ireland and especially in Templemore. We blamed anything and anyone for the fact that you had left and never returned to your family.'

Oliver said nothing.

'And that is not all. Because of you, we took abuse from other children. They teased us because we had no Daddy. They laughed and jeered at us.'

Silence.

'But do you know what?' Kitty continued, no longer caring whether or not he spoke. 'In the end it was all down to you and what you wanted in your life. You wanted another life, another woman, and other children to call you "Daddy". If only we had known what sort of person you were, life would have been different for us, because we would have had more no longing for you. We would have known you were not coming home to us and we would have moved on with our lives long before we did. And, knowing that our mother would be a nobody for the rest of her life, we could have helped her in a different way.'

Oliver looked at Kitty and his lower lip trembled, but he remained silent.

'If we had known about your life here in America, we would not have woken at night crying because we feared that you were dead. Some of us had memories of you and we would have let them go if we had realised what a shit you were. You destroyed our mother's life and you destroyed the childhoods of six children who never stopped waiting for you to come home and who never stopped loving you. And do you know what? Nora, Mammy, was never all right. To her last day she remained unable to function as a human being. She talked about you and longed to know if you were waiting for her at those pearly gates.'

Still nothing.

'Have you anything to say?'

Kitty looked intently at her father. He was thin and clearly very unwell. She felt no pity for him. She was glad he was sick. Perhaps he would die soon. She hoped that he would die roaring.

Kitty took out a pack of cigarettes and lit one. She looked at Oliver long and steadily.

'How could you tell your family that we had all been put in an orphanage? How could you lie to them, knowing that your wife was on her own with six children? How could you leave us to survive on our own in a land where there was no work, no food and nobody to help us? You can't have a caring bone in your body. Well, we defeated you. When we were growing up, we were never separated from each other for more than an hour. And, as I told you, every night – every *fucking* night – we all got onto our knees with our mother, to pray for you, for a father who was now with another woman and had another family.'

Tears flowed down Oliver's face and he raised a hand to wipe them away.

'Look at you, with your crocodile tears. It's too late to cry now. We all cried for you when you left and promised to return, and much good did it do us.'

Suddenly exhausted, Kitty sat down on a chair nearby and looked at the old man sniffling pathetically in his wheelchair. She looked at his rheumy eyes and his trembling lower lip. He seemed none too clean; a stale smell emanated from him. Dried mucus was caked in the corners of his eyes and under his nose.

Kitty looked around the room and took stock of her surroundings. The apartment was neither comfortable nor welcoming. It told her nothing about the life that Oliver had led in America. She tried to assess how she felt and detected no sorrow or any of the emotions she had expected to experience in this moment. She just wanted to be sure of her feelings. Was there anything that she forgotten to say? She did not want to leave anything out now that she was here because she felt nothing but hatred for this pathetic man who had married again and had another family. She did wonder if he had had a good life and if his unlawful second marriage had been a happy one, but she did not intend to ask him.

'I'll go now,' she said, rising suddenly from the chair. 'You'll never see me again. I have no interest in you. I just came to see the man my mother married.'

She opened her bag and took out a ring: Nora's wedding ring. She held it up. 'My mother wore this ring until the day she died. She was always faithful to you, for all the good it did her. She used to say that she had promised to love, honour and obey you. But you, the man she married, did not deserve even a fraction of her fidelity.'

She was sure, finally, that Oliver was a nothing and nobody. He had been of no use to any of them. Kitty put the ring back into her bag.

Faintly, Oliver pointed at the trophies on the sideboard.

'Take some of those with you,' he said, 'and give some to Betty.'

'I will do it for Betty, not for you.' She took one of the smaller trophies and put it in her handbag. At that moment it struck Kitty forcefully that her father had displayed no interest at all in any of her other siblings. With the exception of Betty, he had not mentioned any of their names.

Kitty turned towards the door. The meeting had not lasted longer than half an hour. She could not bear to look at him for a moment more.

'Will you come again?' Oliver asked.

'Never to see *you*,' Kitty said without so much as turning her head. 'And if I do come this way again, I will visit your grave and piss on it.'

Back she went up the short corridor to Oliver's front door. The woman was nowhere to be seen. She opened the door, went out, and then turned to shut it firmly behind her. She crossed to the lift, unaware of her surroundings, mind whirling, feeling no emotion at all. All she could think was: that back there, was it all a dream?

When the lift doors opened she walked straight into her husband's arms.

Arthur could tell that Kitty did not want to talk about what had happened upstairs. He knew that she would tell him everything in her own time. Arm in arm they left the building and Arthur hailed a taxi. Kitty was quiet for a while, happy to be at her husband's side.

Back in their hotel room Kitty sat down, lit a cigarette and poured a glass of whiskey on the rocks for herself and water for Arthur. She looked at Arthur with an eyebrow raised.

'Mission impossible? *Possible!*'

That night as she lay in bed Kitty considered whether or not to go and see her father again. She was still angry and felt that she had not adequately expressed her feelings. It was a long and restless night, but in the end she decided against a second trip. She had done what she had come to do, she had made her point and now it was time to start trying to make peace with what had happened and get on with the rest of her life. She knew that, now that she had found her father, she would never feel the same way about him again. She had finally told him what she felt he needed to know. His children, most of them, were alive and well despite his best efforts. She did not care if she had distressed the pathetic old man. In fact she hoped that the shock of seeing her would shorten his life. He must have wondered over the years whether any of his children would come to find him. Well, now he knew.

*

After Kitty had left, Oliver and his partner, Anita Elizabeth Barry, talked for many hours about the events of the day, their voices hushed and frightened.

'What will we do now?' he asked. 'They know where I am. They'll want me to leave them something in my will. Perhaps they'll all come over to America and make life miserable for me. Who knows what they might do, or what they might want from me, as I don't know any of them. I don't know what they turned out like, or what they are likely to do. I don't know what are they capable of but, to judge by that one, it could be murder. How did she ever find me?' Now that he had met Kitty, Oliver was quite sure that he had no wish to meet any of the others.

Panic set in. For years Oliver had convinced himself and Anita that he had disappeared without a trace. It had never occurred to him that his children in Ireland might want to see or visit him in Chicago. They were all so far away and, as time went on, they imagined that he had simply been forgotten. Back in Ireland Kitty had often hoped, angrily, that her father lived looking over his shoulder to see if his children were coming to seek justice. This, alas, had not been the case. But Oliver was certainly frightened now. On that dark night while they were considering their next move, he even wondered if he had become wheelchair-bound as a punishment for what he had done.

And what if the authorities discovered that he had not been legally married all these years, but was a bigamist? Oliver was afraid that he might have to serve time for bigamy and, as an old, wheelchair-bound man, he did not relish the prospect. And so Oliver and Anita left Chicago and went to Texas, where their daughter was living. There he spent the final years of his life in anxiety and distress, worrying every day that another of his abandoned children would find him.

But, unlike Kitty, the other children from his first marriage had no interest in visiting him or hearing from him. They still felt the hurt that he had caused them and tried to forget him. Kitty continued to dream that, one by one, they would all visit Oliver and frighten him even more, but she knew that they had not shared her obsession of many years. And they all knew that Oliver already been told what needed to be said – she had said it for all of them. The story ended here.

Perhaps some of Kitty's siblings sometimes privately wished that they might visit him just once before he died and have a real memory of what he looked like, instead of just the memory of the portrait hanging on the wall in the front room of their house in Templemore – but if they did, they never mentioned it.

As for Kitty, she was deeply satisfied that she had finally managed to see her father, but she regretted that Nora was no longer alive to hear the tale of how she had hunted him down and given him a piece of her mind. How Kitty longed to sit down with her mother and tell her how she loved her and how she had been the best mother any child could have had, because none of the hardships and difficulties they had faced had been her fault. It would have been the sweetest thing for Kitty to tell Nora how she had found Oliver, how she had told him how badly he had mistreated his family and how very unhappy he had made them all.

It would have put Nora's mind at rest and stopped her from obsessing about him, as she had in the years before her death. If only Nora had known that she had done the best she could for her family, she could have stopped worrying about Oliver and wishing to see him after her passing. He had never been worth a fraction of the sorrow and distress that he had caused his only lawful wife. Worst of all was the fact that, although angry and bitter, Nora had never stopped loving Oliver and, had she been alive, would probably have wanted to see him and forgive him.

Also, now that she had seen Oliver for herself, Kitty felt that she had some idea of the pain her mother had endured over the years. Childhood memories came flooding back and she struggled to banish them. Although nothing would ever make up for the loss of a husband and a father, she felt that she had done what her mother would have wanted and hoped that somehow, somewhere, Nora knew what she had accomplished.

'Now, Mammy,' Kitty said aloud as she was boarding the flight back to England, 'The bastard was alive all the time, he was not sore or sorry for us back home.'

14

Moving on

Kitty and Arthur returned to work in the busy post office in Leicester. Kitty had made friends with many of her customers and they knew that she had gone to America to find her father. People had been talking about her mission for weeks and everyone wanted to know what the outcome of her trip had been. Kitty recounted the story many times and everyone congratulated her for having had the courage to stand and face the man who had made her childhood so very unhappy.

Despite her feelings of accomplishment, Kitty was still haunted by what had happened in Chicago. For months she felt anguish over the fact that the man who was her father had lived in America for years without telling anyone that he had a family at home in Ireland. How could he have let so many Christmases and holidays pass by? Had he ever loved Nora at all? Later, Kitty would learn that Oliver had been disowned by almost all of his sisters and brothers because of his extreme selfishness. Only his younger brothers, John and Mertie, allowed him to visit their homes, although they had never seen fit to tell Nora where he was.

Not long after their trip Arthur and Kitty moved into a new, big house in a residential area in Leicester. It was a beautiful home, with lovely gardens to the back and front where Arthur loved to potter, spending hours upon end in his greenhouse and in the garden. Like Kitty's grandfather, years before, Arthur produced beautiful roses. He even bred a new, purple rose that he sold around the world, making a lot of money and earning him considerable fame in the field.

Kitty, who was more practical, composted the household waste and used it to grow fresh vegetables: lettuce, broccoli, turnips and tomatoes. Every evening on returning from work, she would cook the meat she had bought in their local butcher and go to the garden to dig up some potatoes, fresh vegetables and salad. In the autumn she prepared many apple tarts and crumbles with the round, rich apples from the trees that Arthur tended. She was enormously proud of her ability to make vegetables grow and often compared her bountiful harvest to her experience as a child in Templemore, when she would go out in the dark night, by just the light of the moon, to find some food for the family in the farmers' fields.

Every Sunday Kitty would make Irish stew, rich with the goodness of her garden, while Arthur and his sister Florrie watched a religious service on television and sang along with the hymns. Kitty spent hours preparing and cooking the dinner, content in the kitchen with her own thoughts, knowing that Arthur and Florrie were happy singing. Kitty did not like religion, having seen for herself the influence of the priests on Irish society and of the teachings of the Church on her mother's constant companions, guilt and remorse. But she could see that their religious faith made Arthur and Florrie happy and she did not wish to force her views on them.

Left to her own devices in the kitchen, Kitty acquired the habit of drinking a glass of sherry as she cooked. Then she started drinking more than a glass. Over time, Kitty started drinking so much that, by the time dinner was served, she was merry. Then she started having another glass before bedtime. Soon she was going to bed drunk more often than not. As Arthur's family was very religious, he did not drink and was not in a position to see the warning signs: Kitty was slowly becoming an alcoholic, as her mother had been before her. It was hard for Kitty to shake off her past. Even though she had finally met and confronted her father, she was still bitter about it. She found solace in drinking. Kitty never dreamed that her drinking might lead to a habit or that she could possibly treat alcohol in the same way that her mother, or even her father, had. To Kitty drinking was a social enjoyment but, on her own in the comfort of her home, drinking was also a way to forget.

*

Monica had matured at a young age. She wore her hair backcombed with lots of hairspray and, whenever she went over to Ireland on holiday, her cousins could not believe how quickly she was growing up. By twelve years old she had a bust and wore a bra, which fascinated Marie who had not begun to develop until she was nearly thirteen. As the years went by Marie watched in fascination as her younger cousin was given everything she wanted and, if she didn't get it at first, nagged Betty until she did.

By the age of fifteen Monica was already going out with boys, although Kitty was not happy about her growing up so fast and warned her continually against settling for the wrong young man too quickly. In spite of her mother's warnings, however, Monica became engaged to her boyfriend, Roderick, when she was only sixteen and two years later Kitty found herself deep into plans for yet another McManus wedding.

This was to be no low-key affair, however, as was the usual style in Kitty's family. It was a huge, slap-up celebration out in the Leicestershire countryside. Monica was beautiful in a long, white satin dress on her wedding day, with a lace hood to cover her head. Her stepsisters, Mary and Bernadette, were her matrons of honour in stunning pink satin dresses covered in pink lace. The bride's parents were reunited for the day in their love for their girl. When Kitty saw her lovely daughter appear at the top of the aisle, bathed in rays of sunshine and positively glowing, she had to fight back tears of joy and pride. Who could ever have imagined that her sad union with Dessie might culminate in such a happy day – a day that everyone involved could enjoy without rancour and with few bad memories? More remarkable – and to Monica's great relief – Kitty actually *liked* her new son-in-law, in spite of the fact that she was notoriously hard to please in this department.

Shortly after the wedding Monica and Roderick moved out to a house on the outskirts of Leicester, which they had chosen because it was quite close to the place where Roderick's brother lived and would be perfect for bringing up children.

For their tenth wedding anniversary in 1979 Arthur gave Kitty a wonderful present: a brand new car. He had the beautiful powder-blue Volkswagen delivered to the door of their home with a red ribbon tied around it. An enormous bouquet of flowers had been left on the driving seat.

When Arthur called Kitty out of the house to see her present, she was dumbfounded and speechless for once in her life. Tears of happiness flowed and she threw her arms around Arthur and gave him a resounding kiss.

Arthur hugged her back.

'Now, my dear,' he said, 'you will have to learn to drive.'

The following morning Kitty searched through the telephone directory to find a driving school. She intended to get behind the wheel and start driving straight away and, as always, Kitty achieved her goal.

Learning to drive in one's fifties is not easy and Kitty had to drive every day to acquire the new skills she needed. She found it frustrating and often uttered her characteristic, 'Well now, Jaysus'. It took her about six months to learn and nearly three years to pass her test. In the process she managed to infuriate anyone who encountered her behind the steering wheel. As far as Kitty was concerned, the other drivers on the road were always wrong and she was always right and she grew tense and frustrated whenever anyone got in her way.

Kitty was still driving with her L-plates when her nieces Mary, Marie and Margaret visited her one weekend. She invited the three young girls on a jaunt to London to visit her brother Johnny, whom they had never met because he had left for England long before they were born. While working in the butcher's shop in Templemore all those years ago, Johnny had finally lost heart in his home town and decided to emigrate to escape the misery of his childhood memories. Only Kitty had stayed in touch with him, since he had been disinclined to go back to Ireland and face his unhappy past. He had joined the Royal Air Force and quickly risen through the ranks. On the way he had met and married Rita, a lovely woman, and they had had two children, Kara and Neil. They had lived a comfortable, ordinary life in a residential area of London and then, one morning when Johnny had been just forty, he had woken with a fierce pain in his chest. He was rushed into hospital and treated for a heart attack, but sadly was forced to take early retirement and was now doing voluntary work for the RAF.

Kitty and the girls left Leicester early, at about eight in the morning. There was little traffic at the start of the journey but it gradually built up as they neared London. The more traffic there was, the more agitated Kitty became. The gears screeched and the car jolted forward as she pressed alternately on the accelerator and the brake. Kitty's nieces were reduced to furtive giggles in the back seat.

'Kitty is doing very well,' the girls reported home to their mother later, 'but she is way too highly strung and the other drivers on the road are lucky to escape with their lives, she gets so cross with them!'

In London Johnny and Rita welcomed their nieces into their home with open arms and words of regret that the family had become so dispersed. Nora was discussed fondly, but Oliver was never mentioned. The following day, Kitty made the return journey. She drove much more smoothly on the way back.

*

Although Arthur was much older than Kitty and his health was gradually declining, the couple enjoyed a wonderful time together in the latter years of his life. They went out to dinners and parties and Kitty loved to dress up in the new outfits that she had to wear whenever they attended a function related to Arthur's role as postmaster. She bought shoes and handbags to match and always had her hair done professionally. For Kitty, who had grown up in such desperate poverty, looking good was a way of slapping her presumably long-departed father in the face. Always generous from the day he had met her, Arthur continued to lavish gifts on Kitty each birthday and Christmas, often presenting her with the most expensive jewellery. Once it was a diamond ring with three stones and a beautiful Rolex watch with a circle of diamonds around the face. Kitty had never seen such a lovely timepiece before. She wondered if it wasn't too much for her to have. Did she really deserve such things?

'Arthur, darling,' she told him. 'You don't have to buy such wonderful presents for me. I have never had anything like this. I am not used to caring for such expensive things. I love them, of course, especially as you gave them to me, my dear. But . . .'

'Kitty, my dear,' Arthur replied. 'You deserve everything. You had such a hard life as a young girl. Now it's time to enjoy the finer things in life. I can afford to buy these things for you and I love to do it. The diamonds mean, "I love you".'

'Well,' Kitty said. 'At least I know that my arm and hand are worth something now, with all those diamonds on them!'

Heartened by Arthur's words, Kitty wore her watch and ring every day.

Her husband had always been a very healthy man who looked after his diet and exercised, and he still seemed fit beyond his years. But eventually old age crept up on him and he felt it was time to retire. By this time Monica, too, was working in the post office with Kitty. Both women left their jobs shortly after Arthur's retirement because the new owner had no interest in keeping on his predecessor's family. Arthur and Kitty settled into retirement and Monica found a job at the dressmaking factory with her cousin Mary. Although it had been painful for them to leave the post office, life was good for Kitty and Arthur who often hopped into Kitty's little blue car and went to the seaside or down to London to see her brother Johnny.

But then sadness crept back into Kitty's life when Arthur was diagnosed with cancer. He was confined to bed, where he spent the final months of his illness being tended by his wife and a home care team. Arthur suffered agonies but he never complained to Kitty or to any of the carers who washed him, changed his bed, and gave him the drugs he needed. It was often suggested to Kitty that Arthur should go into hospital but she was determined to take great care of him until the very end. They had been married for well over ten years and those years had been the happiest of Kitty's life. She had never felt a love so strong as she did for Arthur and she would not abandon him now.

There came an evening when she was quite sure that Arthur would not last until morning. She stayed with him all night, holding his hand and accompanying him on his final journey. In the morning, when he took his last breath, Kitty called the health services and then she went out into the beautiful garden Arthur had made, sat on the swing he had built, and sobbed her heart out.

Despite Kitty's sorrow it was an immense relief that Arthur had passed away as peacefully as he had lived. One of the last things that he had said before he died was how sorry he was for becoming ill so that he would not be with his beloved wife in her old age.

'I wanted to be the one to take care of you, my dear,' he told her sadly.

Always a gentleman, Arthur himself had made all the arrangements for his funeral, ensuring that everything would be in order when he passed. He had wanted to save Kitty the effort and misery of having to find an undertaker and make decisions. To Kitty's disappointment Arthur's sons stepped in and organised the funeral without much concern for what their father had wanted. Deeply distressed and not wishing to upset them, Kitty went along with what they had in mind. She was sad that they did not wish to follow their father's instructions, but she was too distraught to worry about what they were doing and the funeral was carried out as they thought fit.

Arthur was laid to rest beside their mother, his first wife. Kitty was devastated by her stepsons' decision not to bury their father in the plot she had bought one year earlier, although she could understand their wish to bury him with their mother. But where did that leave *her*? When she died, where would she be buried? Kitty consoled herself with her belief that she would be with Arthur on the other side.

*

Arthur had accumulated a large sum of money and he left most of this to Kitty, together with their beautiful home. Kitty would be financially secure for the rest of her life.

Now that Kitty was a widow, Monica did all she could for her mother, assisted by her cousin Mary, who still lived in Leicester. They both felt strongly that Kitty, who was relatively young, should get back to work and normal living as soon as possible. It would do Kitty no good to sit and brood in her empty house.

Only a week after she had started to look for a new job, Kitty found a post as a clerical employee for Leicester

City Council, working alongside another Irish woman of a similar age who introduced herself as Jane from Mayo.

Jane had been married twice, each time to an English man, and both marriages had ended badly. 'I'm having no more to do with the English!' she confided in Kitty. 'I'm on the lookout for an Irish bloke now.'

Jane, the youngest of ten children, had been living in Leicester for years without ever having returned home to Ireland. By now, most of her family were dead and gone and she had even less reason to return than before. Despite this, Jane retained her accent and a strong sense of Irishness. Whenever one of Kitty's relatives rang, Jane always asked them to sing 'The Boys from the County Mayo' down the telephone, as she listened, laughing and crying at the same time.

Soon the two women were as close as if they had been friends all their lives. On Friday nights they always went out for a meal and then to the pub. On Sundays Jane visited Kitty in her home. Kitty taught her how to garden and showed her how to grow her own vegetables and salads. She encouraged Jane to buy a greenhouse and visited to help her plant up her vegetable plot. 'I've come to check up on your garden,' she would say every time she arrived.

Partly because of the great friend she had found in Jane, Kitty loved working for Leicester City Council and she began to be happy again, although she would never stop missing Arthur and the wonderful life that they had had together. She was deeply grateful that they had been granted so much time to enjoy one another. Her job, serving all the old women who came in for their bus passes, was a lifeline. It was always a laugh a minute with Kitty behind the desk.

In London, Johnny was not doing well. He had taken good care of himself since his earlier scare, carefully following his doctor's advice with regard to medication, diet and daily exercise. But his condition continued to deteriorate in spite of his best efforts and then, one morning when he was in central London for his usual check-up, he collapsed outside the hospital and died. He had suffered a second massive heart attack and there was nothing that could have been done for him.

Shortly after Johnny's death Kitty went to Ireland to get a sod of turf from the bog in Templemore. Johnny had returned to Ireland only once, for a niece's wedding. He had played the accordion and sung, but had stayed for only two days. While none of the family in Ireland had known Johnny well enough to mourn him very deeply, they could see that his death had left poor Kitty very shaken.

Later, when Marie was visiting Kitty in England, Kitty brought her to Johnny's grave and saw to her satisfaction that the sod of turf was still there.

'He knows he is in touch with his home in Tipperary while that turf stays there,' Kitty said.

Kitty seemed to have become reconciled with her past and now made sure that she visited Ireland twice a year to see Betty. The whole family always looked forward to these visits, as Kitty was such great fun. How everyone laughed at her characteristic, 'Well now!' whenever anything went wrong. But unfortunately Kitty's family also noticed that she had begun to drink more heavily than they would have liked. At first Betty did not mind Kitty drinking, feeling that it was nobody's business but her own, however her husband, Noel, was strongly opposed to letting Kitty have too much to drink in his home.

'Hide your glass, Kitty,' Betty would urge. 'I don't want Noel to see that you are having a drop. That's your third glass, too. Don't you think that maybe you have had enough?'

'I am old enough to have a drink,' Kitty would retort. 'It ain't eatin' anyone's bread.' But she did as Betty asked and hid her glass.

Gradually Betty began to worry more and more about Kitty, whom she loved dearly, and she and Marie made sure to go over to England more regularly to keep an eye on her. On one of these visits Betty and Marie met up with Betty's son, Walter, who had left home when Marie was about nine and was now living in Birmingham. Betty was very proud, emotional and excited to see Walter, who was not very good at writing letters and did not communicate frequently. He had not been in Ireland since the age of eighteen and now he was in his forties. He was as tall and skinny as he had been as a boy and looked like a hippie with his long hair and wry smile. Walter was married to an English girl called Barbara. They had three daughters and a son named after his grandfather, Noel, but the marriage was not going well. Not long after the visit Walter and Barbara went their separate ways and Walter found himself struggling on his own with a drinking problem, like so many of his relatives before him.

Alcohol had now become Kitty's constant companion and it seemed that she could no longer manage without a glass in her hand. She was a maudlin drunk. Sometimes, in the evenings, she would get nostalgic and recall that fateful day when she had met her father and given him a piece of her mind. Her listeners would be forced to hear every detail, over and over again, until they felt they had taken each step with her. They always made the appropriate comments in all the right places. After exhausting that subject, she would move on to the way in which Arthur's family, aside from his sister Florrie, had never accepted or respected her, and dwell morosely on the details of his funeral. 'The thing that upsets me the most,' she would say, 'is that there is no space for me in that grave. There is nowhere for me to go when I die. I won't belong anywhere.'

Everyone could see that Kitty's drinking was a growing problem, but she was clearly a functional alcoholic. Her job at the City Council offices continued to give her something to get up for in the morning and the alcohol never stood in the way of her social activities. She talked at length about the problems caused by her parents' addiction, but she would always deny that she had a problem herself. She thought she could handle it because she was always quick-witted and had a memory second to none. Those talents certainly made her perfectly suited to her work at the City Council where she needed to be able to think and act quickly. Helping those old dears out with their bus passes gave Kitty's family and friends hours of fun, because she loved nothing better than to come home and recount the latest drama to someone or other on the phone, reducing her audience to helpless tears of laughter in the process.

*

Soon Kitty had a more important reason to persevere than just her job. Monica was expecting her first baby. Throughout the pregnancy Kitty made sure that Monica called by each day; she would cook Monica a meal and listen attentively while she reported on her progress. When it finally happened, the birth of Monica's baby boy was a difficult one, but Kitty and Roderick were with her throughout. Kitty's excitement at being a grandmother was a joy to witness. She lavished gifts on the new baby and, although Monica chose everything herself for the baby's bedroom, Kitty insisted on paying. This baby's life was going to be perfect.

Six months on, when mother and baby had settled happily into a routine, Kitty decided that it was time to visit Ireland again and this time she was determined to bring her sister-in-law, Florrie.

Kitty and Florrie had become very close since Arthur's death, in spite of their different personalities. Florrie was timid by nature, but she enjoyed the excitement and adventure the younger woman brought into her quiet, solitary life, which she spent pottering in the garden or walking to the nearest shops and chatting with her neighbours. She admired Kitty's spirit and willingness to tackle almost anything, often remarking that she was lifted up by Kitty's sense of humour and antics and that she had never met anyone quite like her before Arthur introduced her into the family. Although she was quite a bit older than Kitty, Florrie had never married or even had a boyfriend. At one stage Kitty suggested to her that she might try to date a nice gentleman, but Florrie found the experience mortifying because she was so very shy. Kitty understood then that Florrie had no interest in romance.

'In any case,' she told Florrie, 'you're too good for any man. You're the kindest person I know!'

Spending time together helped console the two women for the loss of the man they had both loved dearly, and Kitty was soon driving out to Florrie's house in the country every Sunday to have dinner with her. The house was tiny and as neat as a pin, as was Florrie herself. It was, however, a little old-fashioned for Kitty, who preferred things to be shiny and new. Old, battered furniture reminded her of her childhood home.

'That kitchen table is gone out with the fog,' Kitty would say. 'Its day is done.'

Florrie would just laugh. 'It's only for me,' she would say. 'It belonged to my mother. I'm very fond of it.'

'Well, how about a new dresser, at least? You should put in a new kitchen, but a dresser would be a good start.'

'I don't need a new kitchen. This one is just fine for me.'

'Well wouldn't it brighten up that kitchen to have new presses built in, and it would make life easy for you, with all the pots and pans you have.'

Although she could never talk her into buying a new kitchen, Kitty somehow managed to convince Florrie to come to Ireland with her and the older woman became quite excited at the thought of the trip to meet Kitty's family on the other side of the water. As the day for their departure approached, however, it became clear that Florrie was extremely nervous of flying.

'How many people do you know who died in a plane crash?' Kitty asked. 'Go on. Think about it.'

'Well, none at all,' poor Florrie had to admit.

'That's an end of it then. I'm sure the Lord has your death planned out for you. Don't worry; I'm sure it won't be in a plane crash. Come on, Florrie. Live a bit!'

When they arrived at Betty's house, Florrie was delighted with the warm welcome they were given and amazed by beauty and tranquillity of the Irish countryside, which suited her quiet nature perfectly. She could hardly believe how still and dark the roads were without any street lamps and, when she was taken one night to look out over Kilkenny at the moon, stars and all the sparkling little lights below, she pronounced it the most beautiful thing she had ever seen.

Her travelling companion's pleasure in a peaceful day did nothing to quash Kitty's natural exuberance, however. Monica was expecting her second baby by this time and

Kitty had promised that she would stay in touch regularly while she was away from home. As none of her relatives possessed a phone, Kitty stopped by a local phone box one evening at a pre-designated time to make her call. Unfortunately there was a substantial queue. Kitty didn't care about the queue. She marched to the top of the line.

'I'm first,' she said. 'It's an emergency. A pregnant woman . . .'

Assuming that one of the women in the car was in labour, the crowd stood aside so that Kitty could make her call.

Florrie enjoyed her time in Ireland, although she often felt a little overwhelmed by all the new experiences. Whenever Kitty felt that Florrie was getting tired, she would tell her a funny story to make her laugh. She was taken to see the sights of Kilkenny, Dublin, Wicklow and Killarney, but was most impressed by Wicklow's Sally Gap. After their trip, Florrie would often ring Kitty to talk about Ireland and how much she had enjoyed her time there.

'If not for you, my dear,' she would say, 'I would never have seen such beauty. You make it so much easier for people to enjoy life. I honestly don't know how you do it.'

'Well now,' Kitty would say. 'You don't need to thank me for anything. I wanted to bring to you Ireland and I did it; as simple as that! You should know by now that when I want to do something, it gets done.'

*

The final settlement of Arthur's estate took some time, but eventually Kitty was left with a generous bequest that allowed her to look at the world through different eyes.

She now had the freedom to take stock of what had happened in her life thus far and what might happen yet. She was sure that she still had many years ahead and she had no intention of taking things easy until death caught up with her. 'The world is a big place,' she would often say, 'and it's going to take me years to see it all, so I have to keep up the pace.'

Soon she was venturing much further afield than Ireland, regularly setting off with friends to tour in the Netherlands, Sweden, Germany and France. Kitty loved the excitement of visiting new countries and experiencing their cultures. More importantly, she found it easier not to mourn the loss of her beloved husband while she was away, although the ache of the empty house in Leicester always pained her on her return. There were a thousand little things there to remind her of how much she still missed him. Still, she knew that life had to go on and only she could ensure that the rest of her years were happy ones.

With this in mind, she decided that she would take a month off work and head for Melbourne, Australia, to see her brother Ollie and his wife, Ethel, whom she had not seen since the early 1960s. When she contacted Ollie and told him of her plans, he advised her to come in the first months of the year because it would be cooler in Melbourne then. Kitty took his advice – she planned for this to be the trip of a lifetime and did not want anything to stand in the way of her fun. Kitty's second grandchild was due around the time of her departure, but Monica insisted that she would be fine without her mother and that Kitty should go. She knew that this trip was very important, for Kitty hoped that in making it she could finally stop grieving for the husband she had loved so very much.

15

New ambitions and frailties

Ollie and Ethel had been living in Australia for over twenty years and were very much Australians. They spoke with Australian accents and felt at home in the warm climate. Kitty was excited at the thought of seeing them, but her excitement was mingled with sorrow that Arthur could not accompany her. She was sure that he would have loved to see Australia and to meet her older brother; he had been told a great deal about Ollie as a boy in Templemore, working those long hours every day to save his family from destitution.

Monica collected Kitty at half past six in the morning to bring her to the airport. She had been packed and ready to go since the night before – the biggest trip of all was coming up. Kitty was not at all daunted by the prospect of twenty-four hours in the air, although she did wonder how she would cope with being cooped up on the plane for all that time, especially without a cigarette. Kitty was smoking heavily now and she really needed her cigarettes when she was tense.

'Never mind,' she told herself. 'I will have a few glasses of wine, eat whatever dinner they serve and then put my head down for a kip.'

But Kitty was too excited to sleep. The flight was long and she knew that she should be tired, but she could not stop thinking of how wonderful it would be to see Ollie after all these years. She watched some old movies on the screen. Then she walked about the cabin to stretch her legs, as she had heard that there was a risk of clots developing. She went into the toilet and looked at herself in the mirror. Would Ollie recognise her? She was quite sure that he would, as she had taken care of herself and looked young and trim for her age.

Ollie and Ethel came to meet Kitty at the airport and take her to their home for a month. As her flight had been delayed, they had already been waiting for several hours when Kitty emerged from customs. Kitty was exhausted and was immediately struck by how hot it was, despite the fact that it was winter in Australia. She stood in the arrivals hall and looked around. Could that elderly man really be Ollie? The elderly man smiled and waved: in an instant the years seemed to fall from his face and Kitty saw her older brother standing before her with his arms outstretched. Neither could have predicted how powerfully they would feel – or how many tears they would shed – when they were finally able to fall into each other's arms again.

Later Ollie and Kitty reminisced about their childhood and chatted about years gone by before bringing each other up to date on all the happenings in the family and the fate that had awaited old school friends. Kitty shared the information she had of deaths and births at home in Templemore. They returned often to the topic of their childhood but Kitty always tried to speak of things in a positive light, as she could see that Ollie had been left with a great deal of unresolved anxiety. Ethel had no interest in gossip about the people of Templemore and she left Ollie and Kitty to their talking while she made dinner and did her daily chores. That first night the long-lost siblings laughed a lot and talked long into the early hours of the Australian morning.

Kitty rose late and discovered that Ollie and Ethel had already prepared breakfast for her. After she had eaten her fill, they took her around their home town to meet all their friends. Ollie had inherited Oliver's easy charm and he seemed to know dozens of people everywhere he went. He had reached a stage in his life when he was able to work only when he had to – rather like his father before him – and while Kitty was there he did not work at all, preferring to relax and help his younger sister enjoy the sights. Despite his resemblance to his father, Ollie had no interest in the man and did not seem to want to hear very much about Kitty's historic mission to see him in Chicago.

'Don't talk to me about it,' Ollie said. 'I don't care if the man is alive or dead. If you had to meet him for your own reasons, I am glad you did. But it's nothing to do with me.'

Kitty felt that Ollie had been very badly damaged by having to assume responsibility as the man of the family years before he had been ready for such a heavy burden. He had never spoken to Ethel about his childhood and she had no idea how difficult it had been for him. What was more, Ollie had no intention of starting to tell his wife about it now and so they only discussed the family's great sadness while they were alone.

Ethel, who was many years older than Ollie, was not in the best of health at the time of Kitty's visit, and so

Kitty and Ollie were often left alone to entertain Ollie's friends. Gradually, as he became more relaxed in his sister's company, Ollie began to open up about his memories of childhood, good and bad alike. In the evening, after a few drinks, Ollie and Kitty would start to sing all the old songs that they remembered hearing when they were growing up in Templemore. They both had strong, clear voices and Ollie's friends enjoyed listening and joining in. There were many such get-togethers. Most of Ollie and Ethel's friends were expatriates who were always very happy to meet someone from their homeland. Kitty was always up for a laugh and a good conversation and, of course, a drink or two – or even more. In Ethel's absence Kitty assumed the role of hostess and made sure that everyone had something to eat and drink. People saw that she was a heavy drinker but assumed that she was letting her hair down because she was on holiday.

'Do you remember our father practising this one?' Kitty would say, and she would belt out Dan O'Hara's 'Ah, sure, here I am today'. Ollie would smile and sing along and sometimes he would even take out his fiddle and a few jigs and reels were played.

During her stay in Australia, Kitty visited Ayer's Rock and the other sights, but mostly she just enjoyed the sunshine, and every day she sat in the sun for hours on end to achieve a perfect tan. This she had to do alone, as Ollie and Ethel were not prepared to risk sunburn. Kitty often went out into the garden without sunscreen or a hat and, being such a chatterbox, found herself in rapt conversation with a neighbour and got more sun than she intended. She shrugged off Ollie and Ethel's 'I told you so,' and returned to her sunbathing as soon as she could.

Before she returned to England, Kitty went shopping for gifts and bought something for all her family and friends, including gold earrings, necklaces and native aboriginal ornaments for her nephews and nieces back in Kilkenny. She decided to go to Ireland just one week after returning to Leicester because she was anxious to talk to Betty about her travels and to tell her all Ollie's news. Those two weeks at Betty's home in the country were punctuated by gales of laughter, as Kitty told the tale of her great Australian adventure. Even when she was talking about her mishaps, she always managed to make every story hilarious and her friends and family would frequently find themselves laughing so hard they cried. Kitty had a unique way of spinning a story – what added to her charm was that she had no idea just how funny she was.

*

Back in England Kitty moved on to her next ambition, which became a serious preoccupation. She decided that she wanted to conduct the London Philharmonic Orchestra. This may seem a strange dream for someone approaching sixty with no experience, but Kitty was determined that she would practise as hard as she could until her ambition had been realised. She acquired a baton and when she sat down to watch television at night she took it out and kept it at the ready on the arm of her chair. Whenever an orchestra appeared on the television, she stood in the centre of her living room floor to conduct. Kitty even wrote to the BBC and told the head of programmes about her dream. Sadly, although he wrote back to her politely, this was one wish that was never granted.

Nevertheless, Kitty continued to practise regularly and with great enthusiasm. Indeed, sometimes her head nearly flew off with the effort of her conducting. When

Kitty had company visiting and had had a quite a few drinks, she would begin to conduct as no one had ever seen it done before. The record player was turned on, the orchestra played, Kitty conducted her heart out – and the sky was the limit. Everyone watching was soon in convulsions of laughter. Kitty loved to perform and would continue until she was exhausted and had to give up and fall into the nearest armchair.

'Well now,' she would say. 'Wouldn't that conducting kill you? It's no wonder those conductors are so well off. With all that conducting, they need to be paid well.'

Not content with her private conducting career, Kitty decided that it was not too late for her to learn how to play the piano and she bought a baby grand, spending a fortune. She also bought a candelabra to go on top, as she felt that the splendid piano deserved some embellishment. After much effort she managed to belt out a few tunes and got a handle on the keys and the basic scales, but she realised that she needed to take lessons in order to progress further. Kitty bought all the sheet music she thought she would like, mostly old Irish tunes and songs that she remembered from growing up in Templemore. Then, with the help of the telephone directory, she found a music teacher and started lessons. Proudly Kitty wrote to Betty to tell her about the progress that she had made and the songs that she had managed to learn through sheer perseverance: 'I want to be like Liberace! I won't stop practising until I have it down pat!'

Every night Kitty lit the candles and started to play her piano beside the French windows of the sitting room. Evening after evening, the practice went on. After months of hard work very little progress had been made. Every day Kitty's colleagues at work would ask her how she was getting on and when she would give them a recital and show them how much she had learned.

'I'll let you know when I'm ready,' Kitty always promised. 'You will be the first to know!'

Then she redoubled her efforts and began to practise long into the night. But, hard as she tried, she never got to grips with more than the basics and never learned how to read music. She could not understand why learning the piano was posing such a problem, as everyone in her family was musical and Nora had often told her about her own talent at the piano as a girl. Finally the neighbours started to complain about the awful racket every evening while they were trying to relax and watch television and the lid on the baby grand had to be closed. So ended Kitty's plans to be the next Liberace. But although she no longer played, she continued to light the candles on the candelabra anyway 'to give comfort to the piano'.

Ordinary life resumed and Kitty was often desperately lonely. Although Monica, Mary and her stepdaughters were nearby, they were busy raising their children and getting on with all the pressures of everyday family life. Kitty still missed Arthur desperately. She had no intention of marrying again, but she knew that she needed some companionship in the house. Kitty had always loved budgies so, one Friday after work, she went downtown to the pet shop where she bought a budgie, a cage, food and all she need for her new feathered friend. When she got home, she put the cage and the budgie beside the patio window, so that the budgie could benefit from the daylight and the sunshine. She gave the budgie her own 'English' name, Cathy.

Soon Kitty had grown enormously fond of the little bird. Cathy was no replacement for Arthur but she was good company. Every night before going to bed, Kitty let

Cathy out to fly around the sitting room, although it was often difficult to get her back into the cage again. 'Well now,' Kitty would exclaim in exasperation, 'Get back into your cage.' What was even funnier was that the little bird sometimes did as she had been told. Kitty always drew back the curtains when she was heading to bed, as she wanted the budgie to benefit from daybreak and the sunrise. She loved to come down in the morning to find the little bird singing merrily away and would always call out 'Good morning, Cathy' to her. After some time the budgie learned to reply, 'Good morning, Cathy'. On her way out to work, Kitty would say, 'Bye Cathy, see you later. Don't do anything wild while I'm at work. You'll have to wait until I come home to clean your cage with the pyramids of shit.'

Despite the fact that Kitty's musical ambitions had been thwarted by cold reality, whenever the LPO came on the radio, Kitty would take Cathy out of the cage and conduct with the budgie perched on the end of the baton. The budgie got so used to this exercise that when the music started she would create a rumpus in her cage, wanting to get out and perform for the orchestra.

*

Kitty's life was quite pleasant at that period. She had a good network of friends and she often met them at the weekends for a meal or to go to the pub for a drink. But on those long evenings that she spent alone, she sat drinking and thinking about her trip to America and Canada. She had thought that she had drawn a line under her meeting with her father and moved on, but now it returned once again to haunt her. Had she said the right things? Had she made a mistake in going over at all? Kitty hoped that the bitterness of her words had caused pain and grief to the old man, but she could not be sure.

Then one evening, having had quite a bit to drink, Kitty found the telephone number of one of her half-brothers in the United States and called him to give him a piece of her mind about how she and her siblings had been treated by Oliver. The unfortunate man had only recently found out about his father's past himself and did not know quite how to respond to the angry, drunken woman on the other end of the line. Kitty told him exactly how Oliver's treatment of her family had impacted them all and how they had struggled to cope with the painful emotions and difficult economic circumstances that had been their father's gift to them. Most of all she wanted to know what life had been like for Oliver's second family, growing up. Had they been hungry too? Had they ever wanted for anything? Kitty did not know what she wanted to hear. What was better, to learn that Oliver had not loved his second family either, or to know that at least one of his families had been all right?

'Oh, it wasn't easy for us either,' her half-brother told her rather defensively. 'We never had any extra food in the house. Dad worked as a roofer and didn't have work all the time. I remember being sent to the local shop for two eggs and some leftover bread from the day before and having to share the eggs between us all, while the bread was so hard we were afraid it would break our teeth.'

'Wouldn't you think that such a bad father could have stopped having babies after the first family?' Kitty said.

Kitty was oddly comforted to think that her father's second family also knew what hunger was, although she was not proud of this emotion.

Now that Kitty had established some contact with her half-brother, she was like a dog with a bone. On most Sunday evenings she would have too much to drink and ring her half-brother in America or her relatives in Canada to rant about her father and how he had abandoned his family to their fate in Templemore. She compared the life of her father's new partner with that of her mother and talked, again and again, about how tough things had been for the McManus family. In the beginning her half-brother or her relatives usually empathised and seemed to feel genuinely sorry about the plight of Oliver's first family many years before, but after a while they just did not want to hear about it anymore. They felt, not unreasonably, that none of it was their fault and that they should not be penalised for the crimes of somebody else, especially someone who had died in 1974. And they definitely did not want to hear the broken sobs of the drunk, elderly woman at the other end of the line.

Kitty started to write letters to Betty and her brothers, endlessly complaining about their father's treatment of them. She raked over the past, bringing up memories that most of the siblings had successfully managed to banish. They had all suffered equally years before in Templemore, but most of them had recovered from their childhoods and got on with their lives. They had recreated themselves and they had made sure that their own children would not suffer as they had done. They did not appreciate Kitty bringing all the hurt to the surface and they worried about Kitty's drinking. It was clear that she had inherited the family curse of alcoholism. Would it blight her life during her declining years? Sadly, it seemed as though Kitty was going to spend her final years still angry, upset and distraught as a result of the actions her father had taken, many years before – and there was nothing that could be done to change this.

Kitty's age was beginning to show. Monica lived nearby and supported her as much as she could and her stepdaughters, Mary and Bernadette, also provided a great deal of support. Keith, Mary's husband, was selfless in the help he gave to Kitty. He dug her garden to prepare it for her beloved vegetables and prepared her greenhouse for her wonderful tomatoes and salad leaves. Kitty was very fond of Monica's husband, too. Roderick came to her house every Saturday to do for her any chores she could not manage herself. He painted and papered and put out the bins and, whenever Kitty was away on her travels, he generally kept an eye on things. Everyone was aware that Kitty was vulnerable in the house on her own, especially because she was often drunk from quite early in the evening. Monica had tried to talk to Kitty about it, but Kitty wouldn't listen: 'Wouldn't you think that at my age and station I would be allowed to drink in peace as I wish?'

Betty continued to visit as often as she could, although now she was less frequently accompanied by Marie, who had a growing family of her own. One year, however, Marie brought two of her offspring to visit their aunt. She was anxious that they should know and love Kitty, as she did. Kitty seemed to have a special rapport with Mimi, Marie's daughter. Mimi was a lively, mischievous child and Kitty delighted in her pranks, encouraging her to get up to more and more.

'Come on, Mimi,' she would say. 'I think if we jump hard enough on the couch, we might just manage to fly all the way across the room! Tell you what: you jump and I'll stand on the other side of the room and catch you when you come flying towards me!'

When Kitty was in Ireland, she made a point of spending as much time as she could with Mimi, offering to babysit so that Mimi's parents could go out. Then she would play with the little girl as if she were a child herself, helping her to dress up in her mother's clothes and high heels, to put on lipstick and to parade like a model on the catwalk.

'Jaysus,' Kitty said whenever anyone remarked on her bond with the child, 'I have more fun than she does. I didn't get to play when I was a child and I'm making up for it now!'

*

Despite everyone's fears and concerns about her health, Kitty kept going. She got up at the same time every morning and always had the same healthy breakfast of a boiled egg, two slices of home-baked brown bread and real Irish butter. Then she started her journey to the offices in the city centre, catching the bus at the end of her street. The bus stopped on the other side of the road and Kitty had to cross a pedestrian crossing to reach it. Kitty was of an age to retire by now but she had no intention of doing so.

One morning Kitty was on the pedestrian crossing when a car came out of nowhere at high speed. The driver did not see Kitty and ploughed straight into her. She was thrown up into the air and landed about forty feet away. Kitty was unconscious when the ambulance came for her and the doctors felt that there was very little hope for a recovery due to her age and extensive injuries, which included damage to the head, a broken pelvis, two broken legs and a broken arm. A priest was called and she was given the last rites there and then on the street, after which she was taken to hospital where the assumption was that she would be made as comfortable as possible so that she could die in peace.

Kitty remained unconscious in intensive care for three days. Monica and the rest of the family were told that she was unlikely to awaken, but wake she did.

As soon as Kitty realised where she was and what had happened to her, she had plenty to say.

'I'm in a bad way. Was anyone else hurt in the accident?'

When she knew exactly what had happened, Kitty's first thought was for the driver who had caused the accident: 'Oh, that poor woman who knocked me down must be in a terrible way, wondering if I am dead or alive!'

As Kitty recuperated, she had the full attention of the doctors and nurses at all times. She entertained them every day with her light-heartedness and they often told her that they were amazed by how cheerful she was under the circumstances. When the doctors came to check on her they sat on the side of her bed and barely got a word in while Kitty asked them how they were, whether or not they were married and had children, how long their hours were and how well paid they were. She was hugely grateful to all the medical staff and repeatedly told them, 'I hope that you are all taken good care of, as I wouldn't be here today without you.' Everyone walked away from Kitty with a smile. Even from her hospital bed she seemed to be able to bring out the best in everybody.

Kitty was a survivor. She often said it was her love of life that kept her going. Between hospital and rehab she was in care for a year, but she was always determined to get well.

'Anyone else would have died on the spot,' the doctor told her family. 'But not Kitty. She's a fighter.'

'Do you think I would let a bad driver kill me?' Kitty sniffed. 'Not a chance.'

Throughout her convalescence Kitty received many visitors and this helped to keep her spirits up, especially as she wasn't allowed to drink or smoke while she was there. She was a heavy smoker by this time and would often have three or four cigarettes before leaving the house in the morning, so she found giving up nicotine no easier than not having a drink – but it did her health a world of good. And she was always thrilled when the visitors came: all her old workmates were regulars and any new arrival was likely to find a crowd already installed around her bed. 'If I had known I was this popular, I would have made sure to have an accident long ago,' she said.

After her injuries had started to heal there followed nine months in rehab, while she relearnt the usual daily, personal things, such as dressing and feeding herself. When she was finally able to go home, she was very nervous about how she would manage, as she was still unable to walk and she felt weak and frail. By now she was an old woman with a long-established drinking problem. It would not be easy for her to regain her strength and fitness.

Monica and Roderick had brought her bed downstairs to the sitting room in the front of the house so that she would not have to cope with the stairs. Betty and Marie had flown over from Ireland to be there for her on her return home. It was pitiful to see Kitty unable to do the things she had always done, but she was kept in good spirits by all the attention from her friends and family.

She refused to use the commode that the nursing staff had installed at her bedside. She proclaimed it a revolting object, and said that she was a lady and that a lady would not go near anything so horrid unless she really had no choice. Instead of using the commode, Kitty would crawl on her hands and knees to the stairs and sit down on the first step. Then she would slowly ascend the steps one at a time, still sitting down, until she reached the top and managed to get into the toilet. She came down the same way. After a week she was able to get to the bathroom and have a bath.

Kitty had not been able to have her hair done for a long while and so Marie set it for her with rollers. It was as white as snow, but as thick and lustrous as ever. Despite the accident and all she had been through, with her hair done she was still a very handsome woman.

Eventually, thanks to her sheer determination and her refusal to be beaten, Kitty was able to walk again. Much more quickly than anyone had anticipated, she was able to look after herself again unassisted. But although she seemed outwardly as self-sufficient and strong-minded as ever, inwardly she felt more vulnerable than she was prepared to admit. And, sadly, she had to retire from her job with Leicester Council. This was the hardest blow of all because it made her feel that she really had lost her independence after all.

*

Kitty was stronger now, but she still had to return to hospital regularly for check-ups. When she felt ready, she rounded up all the doctors and nurses who had looked after her and invited them to a party she was throwing in their honour, to say 'thanks' for all they had done. That night her house was overflowing with the staff from the hospital, including their wives and husbands. Kitty wanted them all to have a taste of something Irish, so she cooked a huge Irish stew, saying that they would remember her for the delicious meal. The wine flowed and the party lasted until well into the night. Kitty even managed to persuade her guests to join in with the singing and taught them some of the Irish songs that she knew so well.

One night not long after the party, Kitty went to bed early, having had her usual few whiskies to help her sleep. The night was dark and there was a high wind blowing straight at her house. She got into bed and read for a while before turning off the light and falling asleep. She always took her handbag up to the room with her and left it on the locker beside her bed. During the night she thought she saw the light go on and off again quickly. She took no notice, but just turned towards the window and fell asleep again. When the morning came she got up as usual and was heading for the shower when all of a sudden she realised that her handbag was missing. Panic set in as all her private possessions were in her bag.

'My whole life is in this bag!' Kitty used to say – and, indeed, it was a very big bag and Kitty always kept it very full. She called the police straight away. When she went downstairs, she discovered the precious handbag discarded at the bottom of the stairs. Her money had been taken and so had all the expensive jewellery Arthur had bought for her during the years of their marriage. Kitty had always kept her jewellery nearby, to keep it safe and to make her feel closer to Arthur. Her precious engagement ring with an emerald stone surrounded by diamonds, and the eternity ring with three diamonds that Arthur had surprised her with were both gone. Kitty was distraught. She wore her rings every day and only took them off at night to place in the handbag for safe-keeping.

'My hands will never look the same again,' she mourned. 'Not without my two precious rings.'

Kitty quickly took stock of her home. The rest of the house seemed to have been gone through, but nothing was damaged.

Frightened, she went into the kitchen to make herself some tea. There she noticed that her back door was ajar. She opened it to see if force had been used to gain entry and found a pile of spent matches on the ground outside.

When the police came, Kitty told them what had happened.

'You're lucky that you didn't wake up when you saw the light go on and off again,' they told her. 'You could easily have been killed in your bed. We've seen this happen time and time again.'

Although she had more secure locks fitted, Kitty remained nervous after the break-in and found it hard to sleep. She knew that she would be unable to defend herself from an intruder if she woke at night and found that she was not alone in her house. A few weeks later, when she did her usual morning check on the doors, she once again found that the back door of her house had been tampered with and that there were spent matches all over the ground. The burglar had tried hard to gain entry and the door was marked with the stick that he had used to try to force his way inside. But, although she was upset, she was also determined to continue living in her own home. Her neighbours and friends kept a close eye on her.

16

Three generations

Kitty still lived in denial of her own drink problem. She enjoyed telling the many funny stories she could remember about her mother's fondness for a 'tipple' and felt that Nora's drinking was justified by circumstances. But when her own daughter began to drink during the day, Kitty was forced to take notice.

Monica had grown up aware of her mother's fondness for a drink when she was socialising. As a schoolgirl she had helped her Granny, Nora, when she could no longer cope after a day's heavy drinking. That had been her first exposure to alcoholism.

After her second child, another son, Monica became ill with a chest infection and a bad cough. She bought a bottle of cough medicine to stop the cough, especially at night. Then she got the taste for it and the way in which it made her feel deliciously sleepy. Monica had a happy marriage, but having two lively boys so close together in age was exhausting. She was also suffering from post-natal depression. The effects of the cough medicine seemed like a blessing, for she was able to sleep at night and to suppress the sadness she was feeling. Monica was self-medicating and, because of this, she didn't ask for help. But every day she looked for more medicine. She would ask her mother to bring a bottle when she was coming to visit; neighbours were asked if they could bring some back for her if they were off into town.

At first no one noticed. She always took care to ask different people to bring back the cough mixture and made jokes about not being able to shake her cold. Things changed when her baby had a fall. Nothing serious happened to him, it was just a bump on the head, but everyone thought that Monica might have been unsteady with the amount of medicine she consumed. Her husband took note and voiced his concern about the empty bottles he was finding everywhere in the house.

When all the people she loved began to warn her of the dangers of her addiction, she promised to quit. She did give it up, but for something much more socially acceptable. Monica started to enjoy a drink in the evening after work. At first spirits were her choice but by the end anything would do. She cleverly coasted along with her drinking for a good while until her husband, mother and friends began to pick up this new addiction on their radar.

By this time she was not just having a drink or two at home after work, Monica was going straight to the pub and spending all her wages. She held down her job in the clothes factory – a job she was good at – quite well. But soon she was not eating after work, just drinking, and she began to look very thin and haggard.

Kitty had asked Monica many times if all was well in her life and she was always assured that everything was well and all good. But when Kitty spoke to Roderick he told her that he repeatedly had to pick Monica up from various pubs after work. He said that, at times, she was hardly able to stand on her own two feet. They were having many rows about the amount she was drinking. He was always begging her to contribute some of her wages to the household or, at the least, to do the weekly grocery shopping. Monica would promise faithfully to reform. But nothing changed – she was consumed by the need for alcohol.

Although Monica loved her husband and two sons she was becoming more distant every day. Roderick had now stepped in as the primary carer for the two little ones. The boys were young, but they knew that something wasn't right when they were frequently told that 'Mummy isn't well and has to lie down for a little while'. Kitty helped Roderick when she could and was loving and caring to the boys. She wanted to ensure that they still had a supportive female in their lives, so she brought them out, sang them songs, and told them stories about their mother's childhood. Monica appreciated the love and attention that her mother gave to her sons, but was in too much denial to admit that her addiction was having any effect on them. She said the boys were fine because they had all they needed. What she didn't realise was that all they wanted was her time and attention.

One weekend Roderick and the two young boys were going away for two days with the boy scouts. They left on Friday evening, with hugs and kisses for their mother. Monica was looking forward to a weekend by herself. Roderick hoped the time alone would be good for her and that when they returned on Sunday she would enjoy spending some time as a family after a relaxing time pampering herself. But Monica had other plans – she had bought two large bottles of vodka to enjoy that weekend. After a number of glasses in front of the television, she went upstairs to bed – taking the bottles with her.

She sat drinking in bed and was unable to get up; eventually she passed out and threw up in her sleep. She was so drunk that she choked on her vomit and died. It was tragic and such a waste of a young life. Monica was only in her late thirties. She was not discovered until Sunday evening when her family returned from their trip.

Kitty was out of control with grief. She kept asking herself how this could have happened to her only child. The thought of her young grandsons deprived of their mother at such an early age was devastating. The only comfort that she took for the tragedy was that their father was their main carer and was so good to them. Unfortunately for the boys, they had already become used to their mother being emotionally unavailable for them, but how would they cope with this?

Kitty spoke to Roderick about Monica's alcoholism and helped with the boys, but she could not come to terms with it. She was afraid that the rest of her family would find out and she dreaded telling Monica's father and sisters. Kitty was proud and wanted to keep Monica's drinking a secret, but when she died the problem became crystal clear for all to see. Three generations of women in the same family, all addicted to alcohol. Nora's situation seemed understandable. Abandoned by her husband, a single mother with six children to feed and no income – drink was her only solace. Kitty had also suffered hardship and justified her drinking by her circumstances.

But how could Monica have turned to drink? Kitty felt that her daughter had led a charmed life: a good childhood with all that she had ever wanted, a mother and father who loved her (even if they were not together), a kind step-father, two step-sisters who doted on her, a happy marriage, beautiful children, and a good job. God had taken the wrong woman – she felt that it should have been her. Kitty was never the same. She was a broken woman whose grandchildren were all she had to live for. She was determined to keep in touch with them.

As a result she was not happy when her son-in-law started to see someone else. This new woman did not seem to have much time to bring the boys to see their grandmother. Although Kitty had to admit that she was good to the boys, she wondered sometimes if the woman had already been on the scene before Monica's death. She couldn't tell and didn't want to know. Reluctantly Kitty accepted Roderick's new partner for the sake of her grandsons. When Roderick finally married her, Kitty had to admit that they seemed happy with their new stepmother.

*

One Saturday morning, without any warning, Betty died. She had been sitting in an armchair after breakfast when she quietly took her last breath. Again Kitty was devastated by loss. So much so that she was unable to go to her sister's funeral, although she rang often and spoke at length of her great sorrow at having lost poor Betty, her favourite sister and confidante. It took Kitty more than a year to recover. Some months after Betty's death, Marie went to see Kitty to bring her some of Betty's personal possessions. As soon as they met at the airport, Marie could see that Kitty had aged a great deal. She had lost a lot of weight and was smoking and drinking more heavily than ever. It seemed that she no longer had her renowned zest for life. The losses had been too great and they had finally defeated her.

During that week Marie and Kitty talked about Betty and how she had died. It was painful to discuss, but Kitty seemed to need to know everything.

'Will you do something for me?' Kitty asked one day, quite suddenly. 'Will you get that notebook and write down all the details I know about the McManus family? One day you will write a book and will need all this information.' She pointed at the black, leather-bound notebook on top of the disused piano.

Marie just laughed. 'Maybe someday I will.' She did not take seriously Kitty's prediction that one day she would want to write a book. But she got the notebook, as Kitty asked, and wrote down the information. Kitty made sure that she got everything right.

After Marie left, Kitty felt very alone. She wrote, 'I miss your company in the house. It's like a graveyard here now. I still miss Monica and think of her every day. I miss her phoning me, I even miss our arguments.'

Shortly after returning home, Marie had to go into hospital. When she returned home, she found a letter from Kitty.

'I've been ill ever since you left England,' Kitty had written, 'but the neighbours are keeping an eye on me.'

When Marie rang to see how her aunt was, she learned that poor Kitty was far from well. The doctor had visited her several times and had given her some antibiotics to take, but still she had an awful cough that resisted every form of treatment. Kitty coughed and coughed, she had not eaten for some weeks and so she was malnourished – although she was still able to have a cigarette and somehow was able to get her hands on a bottle of whiskey, without which she was unable to sleep at night.

Social Services brought her dinner every day while she was sick, but Kitty would not eat any of it. 'It's like something a dog would leave beside a lamp post,' she said. She longed for some of her own Irish stew, which she sometimes ate twice a week in winter. Nora had made good stews, too (whenever she could get her hands on good ingredients), and Kitty had learnt well from her mother: home-grown vegetables and prime beef, nothing but the best.

After some time convalescing and taking care of herself, Kitty seemed to improve. She started to go out into the garden to tend to her precious flowers and vegetables and to take little walks down the street where she lived. One day she decided to take her regular bus into Leicester, although she was out of the habit because she had been so weak recently. As she was feeling so well that morning, she did a little shopping, then went to her usual café and had a cup of coffee before heading to the market. Kitty loved the market, especially now that she had retired, and she had made it part of her daily routine to stroll through, admiring the stalls with their wonderful materials: silks and chiffon and cambresine. Still a stylish dresser, she often bought some cloth and had a lovely dress made for herself.

It took an hour to walk through the market but, vast as it was, Kitty knew most of the stall owners and every morning she had a word for them all.

'Morning, duck,' they would always say in return. 'Are you alright, my duck?'

On this particular day, after visiting the market, Kitty posted a 'get well' card to her niece, asking if she was feeling better and how the children had coped with her absence. After popping the card into the local post office, Kitty got on the bus again and made her way home.

That night Kitty thought about her day as she had a few glasses of whiskey and smoked her beloved cigarettes. She was pleased that she had made the short journey into town on the bus, although she had been quite frightened at the prospect before embarking on the trip. At about ten she went upstairs to take a bath in preparation for bed.

As Kitty dressed after her bath, she suddenly felt unwell. She grasped the side of the bath to steady herself, but her time had come. Kitty fell heavily and was gone in an instant.

In the morning Kitty's home help came to visit her. When nobody replied, she called the police who forced the door open. They found Kitty lying over the bath, having died very suddenly at seventy-two years of age.

While Kitty's past had been adventurous, she had still had a great deal left to live for. She had been looking forward to her future with her grandchildren. She had loved babysitting and taking care of her grandsons. She had hoped, when they were older, to tell them all about Nora and about her childhood in a small town in Ireland where their ancestors came from. She wanted them to know about their family and how they had survived without the father who had abandoned them. Who would tell them now?

Possibly realising that the end of her life was in sight, on her previous and final visit to Templemore and Kilkenny, Kitty had brought some of her personal things to give to her nieces and grand-nieces. She had dispensed jewellery and ornaments and, for her fourteen-year-old grand-niece, some special towels for her bottom drawer, all tied up with a ribbon. She told everyone proudly that she was going to leave her beautiful house on a hill in Leicester to her two grandsons.

Kitty had also gone with Marie to see Betty's grave. On the way to the graveyard the car radio had played 'The Isle of Inishfree'; a beautiful old song that tells the story of the generations of Irish people who left their homeland in search of work abroad and how so many died in foreign lands. As the song ended Kitty started to cry and shake uncontrollably. In part it was the song, which could have been telling the story of her own family. She also bitterly regretted the fact that she had not had time to say 'goodbye' to her beloved sister. She told Marie over and over that she knew Betty would look after Monica in Heaven, that they'd be there for each other. When they reached the graveyard, Marie helped Kitty to the grave-side where she fell on the grave and sobbed for a full twenty minutes.

When the time came to leave, Kitty looked up to the sky. 'If there is a God up there,' she said. 'Please take care of Betty for me.' She turned and walked away in silence with her head hung low. Kitty, Ollie and Richard were the only children left now, each living in a different country.

*

A few days after she died, Marie received the get well card that Kitty had posted from Leicester. Even after death she had been able to make her point and it seemed to Marie that her aunt was truly communicating with her from beyond the grave. Perhaps it was a coincidence, but Marie rather thought not. Perhaps Kitty really did have special powers, as many had suspected in the days when she read fortunes. It was a great shock to get a hand-written card after the funeral with many details about how she was feeling that day and questions about how her extended family was doing in Ireland.

In the years to come Marie often thought about Kitty's card. How typical of her to be able to arrange it so that her words would be read after she had departed this world. Had this been Kitty's way of letting her family in Ireland know that her time had come and that she had accepted it?

'If there is a way of communicating from the after-life,' Kitty had often remarked to her niece, 'I will find it, you can be sure of that. If not, well then that's it.'

In death, as in life, Kitty was no ordinary woman.

The likes of her will never be seen again.

Postscript

A family reunited?

About two years ago, eleven years after her death, I started thinking about my Aunt Kitty. I had always wanted to write and I was interested in writing from the point of view of Kitty, who had always been such a strong character and a real touchstone for our family. I was also fascinated by Kitty's father, my grandfather, Oliver. I knew that he had abandoned his wife and six children at a time when a woman alone in Ireland had no real way of making a living and had often speculated about his motivation. It is no exaggeration to say that his behaviour has had a ripple effect through generations of our family.

I suppose that, most of all, I wanted to understand why Oliver went to the States and never came back for his Irish family. As a parent myself, it is very difficult to understand how any father could do something so final and so cruel. I began researching my ancestors, gathering all the details that I could. I was fascinated to learn that records are now readily available online. This meant that I could look up a huge amount of information on the internet. What nobody could ever have imagined was that technology now allows Oliver's many ancestors to trace his footprints. I could trace him crossing the border between America and Canada, and back again, together with his American children and his partner. After all these years all the details are there for anyone who cares to look.

You are caught now, I thought, when I looked at the information on the screen. Little did you think that even crossing the border would one day be public knowledge. It was while looking at these records that I added up the dates and realised that my grandfather's second 'wife' had been pregnant before he came back to get the family passports for Nora and her children and to ensure they were vaccinated. Of course, he may not have known that his other woman was pregnant until he returned to America. No one besides Oliver can ever know the real reason why he did the things he did.

The internet is a marvellous resource. Everything is there for anyone who is interested: details of Oliver's army records, when he fought for England in France, even his sign-up papers bearing his own signature. It is all available with the click of a button. If this resource had been available years ago, Kitty would have found Oliver much earlier. Perhaps nowadays it is harder for fathers to abandon their families. Today we are all traceable.

We now have so many relatives in Canada and America that it is almost impossible to contact them all, although I have been in touch with many. Most of them are very interested to learn of their new relatives and anxious to get to know us. Few, if any, know about Oliver and how shabbily he treated his first family in Ireland.

The first contact was the most difficult. I came across the details of a Nora McManus, from Templemore, County Tipperary. When I looked into this, I found out that she was a grand-aunt, one of Oliver's younger sisters, who had emigrated to Canada in 1926. Her older sister, Kate, was already in Ottawa. With this information, I could ascertain that rest of the McManus family had emigrated en masse in 1930 and even the name of the ship they crossed in. From there, I was able to trace everybody else.

Subsequently, I have been in contact with my grandfather's second family. His eldest son in America, Thomas Joseph McManus, was seventy-seven years old in 2009. Perhaps understandably, he is not forthcoming with much information about his younger years living in America with his parents. I have asked him what it was like growing up in the States in the 1940s and 1950s, but he has said that it was a long time ago and that he cannot remember. Nor has he been able to send me any photographs of his father, my grandfather. It would be nice to think that he and his sister, Neldine, had a good childhood with plenty to eat and drink, that they were never hungry like the half-brothers and sisters in Ireland whom they never knew, but perhaps that was not the case. Oliver seems to have been a poor father to all his children, although at least his children in America did not have to live for years in uncertainty as to whether or not he would ever come home at all.

My research has shown me that many of the McManuses who left Ireland went on to have tough lives, even in the New World. Oliver's younger sister, Kathleen (Kate), who was the first to go to Canada, married a Canadian Mounted Policeman who tracked people lost in the snows of the mountains. Her younger sisters all married in the same area. Nora McManus married a man from Limerick by the name of Smith and went on to have four sons. When he died young, Nora worked three jobs every day to support her family and pay the bills. She worked for the government offices from seven every morning of the week. Her job was to get down on her hands and knees to wash the corridor floor. It was so wide and long that it took the whole day to wash and clean from beginning to end. Then she changed her uniform and went on to clean offices in the same building. At night she washed and ironed for local people. Somehow, Nora survived all this hard work to remarry a man called Whalen when she was fifty-two years old. By this time her sons were almost grown and ready to work. I have made contact with one of Nora's sons. Jeff, who is now getting on in years, is a retired bus driver in Ottawa.

And what became of the rest of the family? Far away in Australia, Ollie's daughter Anna married Martin O'Sullivan, a classical music writer for the television show 'Boys and Girls'. Together with their two daughters, they moved to another part of Australia and joined a religious cult. They all had to be vegetarians and live a simple life, and the women had to cover their hair and abstain from wearing make-up. They lost contact with Ollie, who was very upset by what had happened.

Ollie – by then seventy-eight, although he seemed much younger than his years – travelled to Ireland in 1998. On the way he spent two weeks with Kitty, just before her death in the same year. His wife Ethel, who was even older, stayed behind, calling him every day during his stay. He was with us in Kilkenny for a while. Despite his years and his very weak sight, Ollie still had a great passion for cars and was able to help my sons get their cars up to speed and go to the races with them. He was always full of stories about his life in Australia.

Then Ollie went to visit Templemore, the home town he had not seen for over thirty-five years, and Richard, the youngest of the McManus family and over ten years younger than his big brother. Richard was then about sixty-six, I guess. He had had to retire at sixty, mostly because of arthritis in his fingers. But he had fixed the saxophone up so that he was able to play on for a few years longer.

Dusk was falling as we entered Templemore with Ollie. All the way there we had talked about his childhood. Ollie had laughed and cried. He was nervous about his return. How would he feel? Nora was dead and gone and he had never met Richard's children who were all now adults with families of their own. Suddenly Ollie broke into awful sobs and we had to stop the car and let him cry. When he was ready we went on again. We drew up outside his childhood home, part of a terrace on an ordinary street in Templemore. Other people were living there now and they twitched their curtains to look at the strange car outside, no doubt wondering why we were staring at their house. We moved on again down the main street of Templemore, took a left at the bottom and headed for Lacey Avenue. We paused at the church for a few moments. Ollie had served there as an altar boy when he had been a child, as had his father, Oliver, before him. We stopped again at the graveyard beside the church and said a silent prayer for his brother Seamus and for any friends and relatives who had passed on.

Eventually we stopped outside Richard's house. Richard was waiting outside. Ollie broke down again as Richard approached the car. Ollie opened the door and the two old men embraced each other. Despite the closeness between the siblings as children, Ollie and Richard had not seen each other for decades.

All that day people came to meet Ollie, including some of his childhood friends. Little children playing on the street stopped to see the man who had come back to visit from Australia. As the night wore on a party started. What a homecoming! Ollie spent four weeks in

Templemore and the local county council put on a special reception for him, which was attended by over two hundred people. Richard played his saxophone with the local band and Ollie, who had not played the violin for years, took up a fiddle and started to play as if he had never stopped. All the old tunes came rushing back to him. The local newspaper men were there. They took photographs and wrote a one page article about his return.

Richard and Ollie spent many days and nights revisiting their childhood. They remembered all their old friends, recalling funny stories from their school days. These people had grown old and many had already departed this world. For Richard and Ollie, as for all the rest of the McManus children, the emotions that they had experienced as a result of their father's departure were still very raw.

When Ollie left Templemore early one morning to return to Australia, he must have known that he would never see his native land again and that he was saying goodbye for ever. He returned to his wife, but continued to keep in touch by writing letters of thanks to all his relatives in Ireland.

A few years later my usual Christmas card to Ollie was returned with 'Deceased' written on the envelope. We were never told how or when he died and I have never been completely convinced that he is dead at all. I tried to contact Ethel with no result. She had been much older than Ollie and well into her eighties by the time he came to Ireland for the last time. But it came as a shock that no one had informed us of Ollie's death.

*

A new generation of McManuses in Ireland, America, Canada and Britain has become interested in its family history. Some of this new generation have come to Ireland and Templemore to walk the streets and down through the park beside the lake. Many stayed just one night and moved on. They have been told a very rosy version of their parents' childhoods in the town.

Most of our relatives in North America seem to know little of the truth about their background. Apparently Ollie wrote to all the McManuses in Canada and informed them that there were no more McManuses in Templemore, so they never looked up anyone if they visited the town. I will never understand why Ollie did that – or maybe he didn't and it was just a lie – after all, Richard and his wife were living there and all five of their surviving children married, settled locally, and have children of their own. Perhaps Ollie was trying, in a slightly awkward way, to save Richard from distress.

I have since found out – and perhaps Ollie knew already – that Oliver's sisters, brothers and parents always knew where he was and, for reasons known only to themselves, chose not to tell Nora and her children. They certainly never sent Nora a letter or money. Once they went to Canada it was as if they were gone off the face of the earth. But they must have known that Nora was destitute; they certainly knew that Oliver had taken another woman and had two children.

I spoke to one of them recently and had the same story that Kitty was originally given: Oliver had told them that Nora put all the children into an orphanage, that she did not want them anymore, she just wanted to drink and smoke and not care about anyone. This was so untrue – as we all know now. It was simply a story that got Oliver off the hook so that he could make his new life with the other woman.

It seems possible that there are also relatives in France. As a matter of interest we, Oliver's descendants, would love to find out for sure – and maybe even meet them or their children or grandchildren. We came tantalising close quite recently to discovering the truth about Oliver's escapades in France during the war. In 2009 a gentleman passing through Templemore stopped one of the local women.

'I wonder if you can help me,' he said, in a pronounced French accent. 'I am wondering if there are any McManuses in the town?'

'Indeed there are,' Nicole said. 'I am a McManus myself.' The lady in question was one of Oliver's great grandchildren.

The gentleman explained that he was from France and that his origins lay in Templemore but that he did not know a lot about his Irish ancestors. He asked for Nicole's telephone number, but has not been heard of since. It seems more than possible that this man was the descendent of one of Oliver's conquests in France, long ago during the First World War.

But for my Aunt Kitty, who made a point of remembering everything and insisted that I write it all down, I would never have known the story of my family – even if we will never know the full truth of everything that Oliver did.

Once again, as the old people still say in Ireland: 'The likes of her will never be seen again'.